Markt- und Unternehmensentwicklung
Markets and Organisations

Edited by
A. Picot, München, Deutschland
R. Reichwald, Leipzig, Deutschland
E. Franck, Zürich, Schweiz
K. M. Möslein, Erlangen-Nürnberg, Deutschland

W0235258

Change of institutions, technology and competition drives the interplay of markets and organisations. The scientific series 'Markets and Organisations' addresses a magnitude of related questions, presents theoretic and empirical findings and discusses related concepts and models.

Edited by

Professor Dr. Dres. h. c. Arnold Picot
Ludwig-Maximilians-Universität
München, Deutschland

Professor Dr. Professor h. c. Dr. h. c.
Ralf Reichwald
HHL Leipzig Graduate School of
Management, Leipzig, Deutschland

Professor Dr. Egon Franck
Universität Zürich, Schweiz

Professorin Dr. Kathrin M. Möslein
Friedrich-Alexander-Universität
Erlangen-Nürnberg & HHL, Leipzig,
Deutschland

Carsten-Constantin Soeldner

Open Innovation in Embedded Systems

With a foreword by Prof. Dr. Kathrin M. Möslein

 Springer Gabler

Carsten-Constantin Soeldner
Nürnberg, Germany

Dissertation Universität Erlangen-Nürnberg, 2016

Markt- und Unternehmensentwicklung Markets and Organisations
ISBN 978-3-658-16388-4   ISBN 978-3-658-16389-1   (eBook)
DOI 10.1007/978-3-658-16389-1

Library of Congress Control Number: 2016956813

Springer Gabler
© Springer Fachmedien Wiesbaden GmbH 2017

Printed on acid-free paper

This Springer Gabler imprint is published by Springer Nature
The registered company is Springer Fachmedien Wiesbaden GmbH
The registered company address is: Abraham-Lincoln-Str. 46, 65189 Wiesbaden, Germany

Foreword

Embedded systems have already for a long time been the hidden champions of a broad variety of electronical devices. While they are already constant companions in our daily lives, only in recent years they have moved to the foreground of innovation. Traditionally, they have been designed for a specific purpose without giving the freedom of changing or growing their functionality throughout their lifecycle. Most impressively, the potential of embedded systems has revealed itself in today's smart phones with their great variety of applications. Step by step we understand that similar developments are also taking place with other classes of embedded system – ranging from cars or utility vehicles to domestic or robotic devices, to name just a few. Firms seeking to innovate are searching for innovative ideas and applications outside the boundaries of their firm – a phenomenon denoted as 'open innovation'. Bringing open innovation and embedded systems together bears a huge potential. Applying open innovation to existing embedded systems assumes that the system is already open to some degree – but usually, embedded systems have not been designed with openness in mind. This leads to a twofold challenge: the technical opening of embedded systems as well as the organizational opening required for open innovation.

Constantin Söldner addresses exactly this complex interplay of technical and organizational challenges. His work sheds light on the question how open innovation can be enabled for embedded systems. Whereas prior studies were focusing on the organizational side of open innovation or were exploring how online innovation platforms can be used to bring together external actors, the focus on the technical product as open innovation platform itself is rather new and exciting.

To illuminate open innovation in embedded systems, Constantin Söldner addresses the following aspects:

- Technical characteristics of embedded systems which constrain and enable open innovation practices
- Organizational forms of openness
- Technical forms of openness
- Modularizations for open innovation in embedded systems
- Open innovation in embedded systems without opening

Thus, the author provides comprehensive insight on open innovation in embedded systems. Researchers as well as practitioners can equally benefit from his findings. His work not only paves the way for further research. It also offers new insights for both researchers from the field of open innovation as well as embedded systems. In conclusion, this work appeals by it practical reach, academic scope and relevance. It has been accepted as a doctoral dissertation in 2016 by the School of Business and Economics at the Friedrich-Alexander University of Erlangen-Nuremberg.

The book is a must-read for all those who intend to conduct open innovation in embedded systems or who want to gain a better understanding on how open innovation can be enabled in a technical context. I wish the book the broad dissemination it deserves.

Prof. Dr. Kathrin M. Möslein

Overview of Contents

Table of Contents

List of Figures

List of Tables

List of Abbreviations

API	Application Programming Interface
ASIC	Application Specific integrated circuits
CAN	Controller Area Network
CCL	Creative Common License
DAM	Data Access Module
ECU	Electronic Control Unit
ES	Embedded Systems
FPGA	Field Programmable Gate Array
GDK	Glass Development Kit
GPIO	General Purpose Input Output
HW	Hardware
IDE	Integrated Development Environment
IP	Intellectual Property
IEEE	Institute of Electrical and Electronics Engineering
IFTTT	If this than that
LAN	Local Area Network
MDK	Module Development Kit
NDA	Non-Disclosure Agreement
OI	Open Innovation
OS	Operating System
OSGi	Open Service Gateway Initiative
PCB	Printed Circuit Board
RACE	Robust and reliable Automotive Computing Environment for future eCars
RBV	Resource-Based View
RQ	Research Question
RT	Real-Time
SDK	Software Development Kit
SW	Software
SoC	System-on-a-Chip
USB	Universal Serial Bus

Part I

Introduction

1 Motivation and relevance

Embedded systems have been for a long time the hidden enablers in almost all kinds of electronical devices. As applied computer systems being 'embedded' inside of a larger system or device, they steer and control the functions electronic devices provide. Often they are subject to a varying set of requirements, like safety, security or real-time requirements (Marwedel 2011; Noergaard 2005). Embedded systems have more and more become ubiquitous, with 98% of all computer chips manufactured for embedded systems (Ebert and Jones 2009). Whereas the general public has not been aware of their importance, with their increasing capabilities and functions they move into the foreground of innovation. Although traditionally, ES have been developed for specific use cases without much room for customization, this paradigm is rapidly changing. In the automotive domain, a survey shows that ES already constitute the requirement for almost 90% of innovation (Fortiss 2011). The current trend towards the Internet of Things and smart objects is also based on embedded technologies like sensors, actuators and processing units. The increasing capabilities of ES to lower prices also drive innovation on this frontier.

Firms already have recognized the potential of ES to drive innovation, but to benefit from it, they require additional capacities and expertise. Furthermore, firms also need to identify additional use cases for their systems. A strategy to overcome these challenges is to involve externals in the implementation of additional applications. An example where this brought extraordinary results is the advent of smart phones. They constitute embedded systems whose functions and capabilities are to a large extent brought from outside sources. In contrast to mobile phones, which offered only limited options to install additional software, smart phones offer a vast number of third-party applications. This has greatly broadened the variety of use cases for smart phones. Smart phones are just an example of embedded systems, which have been traditionally developed in a closed fashion, but are now opening up for outside innovation. This development towards opening for outside innovation is reflecting a greater trend which has been coined open innovation in the literature (Chesbrough, 2003).

While smart phones were one of the first kinds of embedded systems which were opened for open innovation, similar trends are visible in a variety of different kinds of embedded systems. Examples for similar trends can e.g. be found in the smart home domain, in the automotive domain, robotics or in digital cameras.

Research in open innovation has already pointed out the benefits firms receive by pursuing open innovation. Besides getting access to a greater pool of potential innovators (Reichwald and Piller 2006), it allows embedded system firms to compensate for missing internal resources and building additional services on top of their systems. Current research in open innovation mainly deals with the opening of the innovation process itself, but does not focus on how open innovation can be implemented in a technical setting such as ES. Open innovation in ES goes beyond 'regular' open innovation in that sense, that externals may not only contribute their ideas but also implement their ideas themselves. To enable this type of open innovation, ES firms need to open their system and design it in such a way that externals would be able to contribute. Thus, in contrast to other non-technical settings, pursuing open innovation for ES not only involves opening the innovation process, but also opening ES as well. In this thesis, opening the ES refers to the notion of providing externals with the possibility to make changes to the ES, i.e. implementing additional software or hardware functionalities.

Openness in the context of technologies refers to the easing of restrictions on the use, development and commercialization of a technology (Boudreau 2010; Shapiro and Varian 1999). These restrictions can be of an organizational, but also of a technical nature. Although open innovation for general-purpose computer systems like PCs or notebooks is already prevalent (Boudreau 2011), embedded systems possess unique characteristics challenging existing practices. First of all, as ES have traditionally been designed for a particular designation (Marwedel 2011), they usually are not designed for allowing open innovation. Furthermore, ES exhibit a variety of characteristics such as dependability (e.g. safety and security requirements) or real-time requirements inhibiting open innovation. In contrast to normal computer systems, ES also make use of a variety of sensors and actuators, which gives rise to different kinds of use cases which are not found in computer systems like PCs or notebooks. Therefore, ES constitute an idiosyncratic setting demanding specific approaches for open innovation. This dissertation aims to tackle these challenges and explore how firms can enable open innovation for embedded systems. This question will be illuminated both from an organizational as well as from a technical perspective. Both these perspective need to take into account the specific characteristics of embedded systems. Thus, this dissertation aims to make the following contributions:

It will extend research in open innovation by expanding its reach to the technical domain of embedded systems. As stated above, pursuing OI in ES often requires the opening of the ES itself. However, there is also the possibility of open innovation without an explicit opening of the underlying ES. Therefore, the first part of the results will depict forms of OI in ES, which are not opened, while the remaining parts will consider open innovation by opening ES.

For OI in ES, which are explicitly opened, both the technical and organizational challenges related with pursuing open innovation in ES will be presented. This will be guided by exploring the applicability of the three core open innovation processes as suggested by Gassmann & Enkel (2004). Furthermore, different approaches towards realizing open innovation for ES, which take into account the challenges encountered in ES will be presented.

This thesis will contribute to research in the field of embedded systems by presenting technical design aspects of ES, which are opened for open innovation. In particular, this thesis offers strategies to modularize ES in accordance with open innovation. Furthermore, another contribution is the operationalization of the notion of openness in the context of ES.

The thesis also holds implications for practitioners as the theme of opening ES is gaining increasing popularity. However, ES firms are typically still reluctant when it comes to opening their systems for externals. Many of these firms are still keeping their systems closed in order to protect themselves from risks involving safety, security and from other potential risks. These risks need to be carefully considered when opening ES. Thus, this thesis aims to illuminate the challenges associated with openness and present ways to resolve them.

2 Structure of the thesis

The present thesis is divided into 5 parts reflecting the research process, which took place in the pursuit of the research aim. Each part constitutes a self-enclosed research step building on the previous parts. A part itself is laid out in chapters, which represent thematic units. To provide further structure, each chapter itself includes sections as well as sub-sections.

Part I introduces the relevance of the thesis' research aim for research and practice. It also outlines the structure of this thesis and gives an overview of the individual parts. Furthermore, it gives a brief summary of what this thesis aims to achieve.

Part II lays out the theoretical foundations on which this thesis rests. First of all, it presents the main topics of this thesis, open innovation and embedded systems and shows their interrelationship. In addition, it also presents the theoretical lenses, which provide the foundation for the later empirical studies. Resulting from the theoretical foundations presented in this part, the research gap is derived.

Part III constitutes the empirical part of the thesis. It begins with the presentation of the research design. The research design presents the research goal and the different studies, which aim to achieve the research goal. Each of the studies is laid out in a separate chapter, following a similar structure: first of all, the research design of each study is presented, followed by the data analysis and the conclusion. The first study constitutes an exception as it is based on a conceptual analysis.

The studies 1, 2 and 3 are tackling the phenomenon of open innovation by explicitly opening ES. This approach to open innovation in ES encompasses the main part of the empirical work of this thesis. The first study explores the three core OI processes in the context of ES by analyzing both literature in the field of embedded systems as well as open innovation. In the second study, the focus is on the organizational openness required for ES. As a foundation for this study, 12 expert interviews have been conducted. The third study deals with the technical openness of ES and the required modularity of ES for open innovation. This study is based on 16 case studies covering embedded systems in different industries and companies. In contrast to the preceding three studies, the fourth study explores the phenomenon of open innovation in ES without opening the underlying system.

A comprehensive discussion of the conducted studies is presented in the fourth part. It overarchingly discusses the results of the thesis' studies towards the overall research question. It also reflects on the research design used in this thesis and shows the limitations of each of the studies. Furthermore, it includes a cross-study discussion, which aims to uncover additional findings when comparing, and validating the results of each individual study.

The last part (Part V) summarizes the thesis and presents the contribution of this thesis, both to research, as well as to practice. Regarding the implications for practitioners, it especially takes into account the implications for decision makers and system architects. It concludes with potential venues and questions for future research.

Table 1 graphically depicts the structure of this thesis.

Table 1   Structure of the thesis

I.	Introduction
	▪ Introduces the relevance of open innovation in embedded systems
	▪ Presents the context of embedded systems and its need for distinct open innovation approaches
	▪ Depicts the structure of the thesis and provides an overview of each part

II.	Theoretical Foundations
	▪ Present the topics open innovation and embedded systems and its interrelationships
	▪ Provides the theoretical lenses which are used for the later empirical part
	▪ Outlines the research gap

III.	Empirical Part
	▪ Presents the research design
	▪ Study I: Explores the three core OI processes in regards of the technical characteristics of ES
	o Conceptual study based on literature in the field of OI and ES
	o Presents the implications of the technical characteristics of ES on the potential of the three core OI processes
	▪ Study II: Explores organizational openness for OI in ES
	o Qualitative study based on 12 expert interviews
	o Presents three forms of organizational openness with corresponding organizational and technical constraints and requirements
	▪ Study III: Explores the technical openness and modularity of open ES
	o Comparative exploration of 16 case studies
	o Provides an operationalization of technical openness of ES
	o Presents modularization strategies for OI in ES
	▪ Study IV: Explores/ Presents cases of open innovation without opening the embedded system
	o Qualitatitve exploration of 8 case vignettes
	o Identifies two forms of OI without opening ES

IV.	Discussion
	▪ Summarizes the empirical research studies and their contribution towards the research question
	▪ Provides a cross-study discussion to compare and validate the findings
	▪ Reflects the research design used in this thesis

V.	**Summary and Contribution**
▪	Provides a summary of the thesis
▪	Presents the managerial and research implications of this thesis
▪	Shows future research possibilities

Part II

Theoretical Foundations

1 Overview

This part aims to present the theoretical foundations, which serve as the basis for the accomplishment of this thesis' research aim. As the goal of this dissertation is to explain how firms can enable open innovation for embedded systems, first of all, the main concepts of embedded systems and open innovation will be presented in chapter 2 and chapter 3.

Chapter 2 encompasses the definition of embedded systems and the presentation of their characteristics. In particular, the specifics of embedded systems in comparison to ordinary computer systems will be explained. These characteristics differentiating ES to other kinds of systems justify the special consideration of open innovation in this context.

The third chapter focuses on open innovation and shows how it can be distinguished from traditional innovation processes. It also emphasizes the specific characteristics of open innovation in ES. As the thesis aims to explore open innovation in ES, the particular constraints and challenges for open innovation in embedded system will be outlined. One of the main propositions in this chapter is that to conduct OI in ES successfully, a mere opening of innovation processes is not sufficient. Rather, it also requires technically opening the underlying ES. This is because traditional ES are often designed in such a way, that externals are not able to make changes to the system. OI in ES, which are not opened, would therefore only to a limited degree be possible. However, systems can also exhibit characteristics, which allow performing open innovation without the ES firms' decision to open their system. To better understand the role of openness for open innovation, this thesis thus distinguishes two forms to OI in ES: *open innovation without opening ES* and *open innovation by opening ES.*

The theme of openness is in more detail elaborated in chapter 4. First of all, a general explanation of openness and its characteristics is provided. Furthermore, the notion of the "degree of openness" is introduced. Moving from this general view on openness to an operationalization of openness for ES, Chapter 4.2 starts by presenting openness in the context of computer systems. Chapter 4.3 then specifically discusses openness in embedded systems. However, to provide a comprehensive view on openness which can be used to analyze OI in ES, sound theoretical underpinnings are needed.

To theoretically elaborate the notion of openness of embedded systems, two main theoretical perspectives will be used: literature on platforms and modularity theory.

The platform perspective will be laid out in 4.4. Platforms deals with systems, which can be extended by other parties building on a core part which is offered by the platform provider. This literature provides insights, how and why a system should be opened to externals. In this regard, the literature on platforms gives insights into strategies behind openness decisions. Of particular relevance is the question, which components of a system should be offered by the platform provider, thus being part of the core of a platform, and which components can be supplied by externals. A crucial challenge firms are facing when opening ES is to determine the degree of openness, which is in alignment with their strategic goals.

The second theoretical perspective, modularity, provides further background for the technical design of open ES. Due to its modular composition, openness of embedded systems not only occurs on the level of the system-as-a-whole, but also requires an in-depth examination of its different parts and the relationship between them. Modularity theory provides the basic building blocks to describe how complex systems are structured and composed. This allows gaining insights, how openness can be realized at different levels of a system (chapter 4.5).

2 Embedded systems

Basically, every device which contains a computer, but is not intended to act as a general-purpose computing system is an embedded system (Wolf 2001). In contrast to general-purpose computing systems, embedded systems usually serve a dedicated function (Noergaard 2005). To fulfill their purpose, ES consist of hardware and software components often designed specifically for the information-processing requirements of the corresponding device (Spaanenburg and Spaanenburg 2011). Embedded systems can be found in a wide array of different fields: e.g. in automotive electronics, aircraft electronics, trains, telecommunication, medical systems, military applications, authentication systems, consumer electronics, fabrication equipment, smart buildings and robotics (Lee and Seshia 2015; Marwedel 2011). Resulting from these broad application areas, ES have to fulfill specific requirements. The requirements posed on embedded systems are dependability requirements (which entails reliability, maintainability, availability, safety and security), real-time requirements and efficiency requirements (Marwedel 2011; Wolf 2001). Furthermore, ES can be characterized as reactive systems, taking inputs from their environment. They consist of digital and non-digital parts (Marwedel 2011; Spaanenburg and Spaanenburg 2011). Often, the software of the ES cannot be changed by end-users (Heath 2002). In addition embedded systems have to be designed to be cost- and energy-efficient (Spaanenburg and Spaanenburg 2011). As a result, ES are typically constrained regarding their hardware capacities, for instance regarding processing capabilities, energy consumption, memory and other hardware characteristics (Noergaard 2005). However, an ES does not have to possess all of the mentioned characteristics to be considered as an ES, but usually ES possess a subset of these requirements (Marwedel 2011). For instance, smart phones are very similar to personal computers as they can be used for general-purpose functions, but can also be considered an ES as their computing parts are designed to fulfill a specific purpose. Therefore, general-purpose computer systems and embedded system cannot always be clearly differentiated, as the example of smart phones demonstrates. The examples of mobile and smart phones demonstrate this fluidity. Mobile phones are an example of ES, but microprocessors in smart phones are not dedicated to a specific application anymore. Due to the high diversity of ES, to be regarded as an embedded system, not all of these characteristics must be present, but a computer system can be classified as an ES, when it fulfills most of these characteristics (Marwedel 2011).

An overview of the characteristics of ES can be seen in Table 2. Although ES can be quite different, because of these common characteristics common design approaches are needed (Marwedel 2011).

Table 2   Characteristics of embedded systems according to Marwedel (2011)

ES characteristic	Description
Dependability	Encompasses reliability, maintainability, availability, safety and security
Efficiency	Can be measured in energy consumption, run-time efficiency, code size, weight and cost
Sensors and actuators	Integrated in the environment through sensors and actuators
Real-time constraints	Computations must be finished in a certain time frame; could be soft or hard real-time constraints
Reactive systems	System execution is shaped by the environment
Hybrid systems	Include analog and digital parts
Dedicated user interface	Realized for instance through push buttons, steering wheels, pedals etc.
Dedicated towards a specific application	Contain specific software which accomplishes a certain task

The characteristics of ES depicted in Table 2 differentiate ES from general-purpose systems and are the reason why open innovation in ES needs to be considered separately. Chapter 4.3.2 will explain these characteristics in more details and show their implication on embedded systems openness.

Another challenge for exploring OI in this setting is that ES come in many different varieties dependent on their specific designation. Thus, ES differ widely in their capabilities. Whereas some ES offer rather low computing capabilities, e.g. are based on an 8-bit microcontroller, which is often used for devices with lesser computing demands, other types of ES have similar capabilities as personal computers.

The design process of ES is also largely determined by these characteristics. Traditionally, ES are designed in a closed fashion where the whole software stack is provided by the device manufacturer. Except for firmware upgrades, the software stack is not altered. In many cases, ES are designed in such a way, that they cannot be reprogrammed after they have been produced or only with great effort. This approach to embedded systems design allows to fulfill efficiency and dependability requirements, however also leads to less flexibility for additional applications. Nowadays, due to the increasing complexity and functionality of ES, they are gradually moving into the direction of general-purpose systems (Aguiar and Hessel 2010; Heiser 2008). For instance, applications originally written for PCs can now be found in smart phones (Heiser 2008). Therefore, one of the characteristics of ES, namely being dedicated only to a specific application does not apply in every case anymore. The use of more general-purpose architectures enables the development of additional use cases for once closed ES.

Another factor leading to more general-purpose systems is due to technical advances. Whereas traditionally, ES are often based on application-specific integrated circuits (ASIC), which are programmed once and keep their initial programming during the systems lifecycle, nowadays ES are increasingly realized with Systems-on-a-Chip (SoC). SoCs often possess heterogeneous system architectures, ranging from completely reprogrammable processors to fully dedicated hardware components. Depending on whether the focus is on flexibility or on optimized performance and efficiency, different designs can be chosen (Pimentel, Erbas, and Polstra 2006).

Such a move towards a more general-purpose architecture finds its expression in the layer model of ES as depicted in Figure 1. The division in specific layers as depicted in Figure 1 is however not exclusive to ES, but also applies to computer systems in general. In its most basic representation, an embedded system consists of a hardware and a software layer, with the software running on top of the hardware. Furthermore, the software layer, however, is usually subdivided in additional layers, e.g. the operating system and the application layer. The hardware layer and the operating system layer offer standardized interfaces which allow the upper layers to access the lower layers' functions. Partitioning a system in such a way is a common approach to reduce the dependencies between the software and hardware, but also between the applications and the operating system.

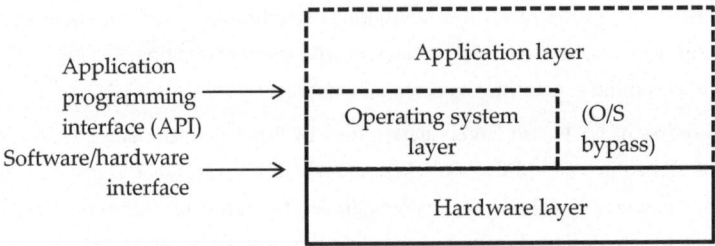

Figure 1   Layers of ES according to Saltzer & Kaashoek (2009)

Although ES which are designated towards a specific purpose are also built according to this layer model, the independence between these layers becomes more prominent in general-purpose systems. This development offers potential for delivering new kinds of innovative functionalities in formerly closed ES. However, to realize this, ES firms have to go beyond the technical realization and incorporate the organizational side as well. This thesis especially focuses on contributions by actors outside of the traditional innovation process. To discuss the particular challenges and potentials of opening ES for external contributions, the next chapter will introduce open innovation and its implications in the field of ES.

3   Open innovation

Open innovation represents a new paradigm how innovation processes inside and outside the firm take place. In comparison to traditional innovation processes, which have been scoped to internal resources for innovation, OI advocates incorporating external parties in the innovation process (Chesbrough, 2003). Chesbrough & Crowther (2006) also describes open innovation as "the use of purposive inflows and outflows of knowledge to accelerate internal innovation and to expand the markets for external use of innovation, respectively". West, Vanhaverbeke, & Chesbrough, (2006) describe open innovation as "both a set of practices for profiting from innovation and a cognitive model for creating, interpreting and researching those practices". The phenomenon of open innovation is neither novel in practice nor in literature (Reichwald and Piller 2005). The concept of absorptive capacity for instance suggested by Cohen & Levinthal (1990) relates to an organizations capability to absorb external ideas and knowledge as inputs for innovations. The notion of open innovation is depicted in Figure 2, which shows both the inflows and outflows of knowledge, and the flows of ideas and rights through the boundaries of a firm.

The concept of open innovation has been further operationalized by Gassmann & Enkel (2004) who proposed three different OI processes: The outside-in process aims to incorporate external ideas, whereas the aim of the inside-out process is to exploit internal ideas outside the boundaries of the firms. The coupled process combines both the inside-out and the outside-in process (Gassmann and Enkel 2004).

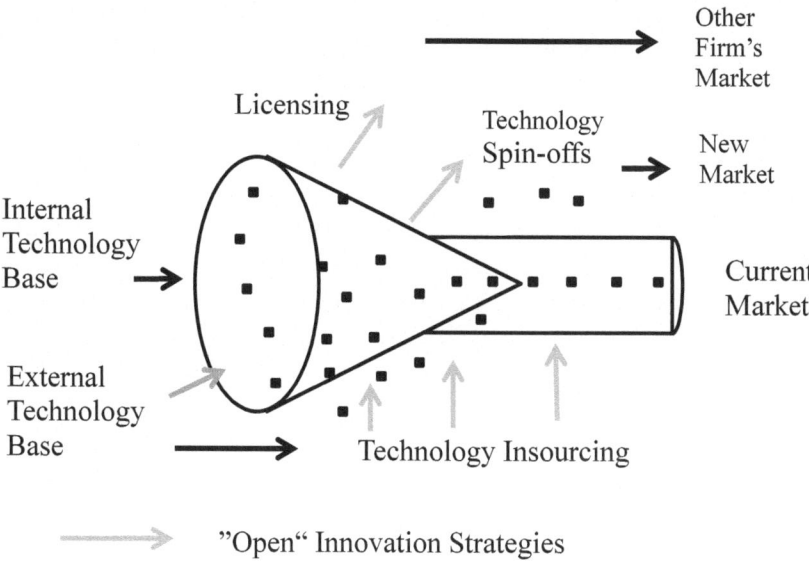

Figure 2   Open innovation according to Chesbrough (2006)

Alongside this more corporate view on open innovation as represented by Chesbrough, there exists a second perspective on open innovation putting more emphasis on emergent open innovation by so-called lead users (Huff, Möslein, and Reichwald 2013). This perspective was brought forward by Eric von Hippel. It takes the view that many innovations are actually developed by self-motivated groups of dispersed actors, often collaborating through the internet (von Hippel, 2005). The foundations of this view already lies in the lead users paradigm coined by von Hippel (1986). A major inspiration for this view on open innovation were the experiences gained from the open source software sector, where principles like technology transfer or the spin out/ spin in of technologies can be observed (Elmquist, Fredberg, and Ollila 2009; Reichwald and Piller 2005). For instance, Gruber & Henkel (2004) explored how new ventures based on open innovation in the embedded Linux market emerge.

Although the second perspective on open innovation is not focusing on the exploitation by companies as Chesbrough's view on OI advocates, it is nonetheless worthwhile for companies to consider the potential of von Hippel's view. For instance, the potential of open source can also be incorporated in a companies' open innovation strategy. E.g. West & Gallagher, (2006a) proposed 4 different open innovation strategies for firms regarding open source software: (1) Pooled R&D, (2) Spinouts, (3) Selling complements, (4) Donated Complements. Thus, although the two views on OI constitute two different paradigms, they still influenced each other.

Open innovation in embedded systems

To put open innovation in the context of this thesis, it needs to be considered how OI can take place in ES. As the last chapter has shown, ES are traditionally designed in a closed fashion where extensibility by externals is usually not a design goal. Rather, for specific kinds of ES, such as safety-critical ES, it is even not wanted. Therefore, in this thesis it will be differentiated between two different forms of OI in ES:

- Open innovation in embedded systems by opening embedded systems
- Open innovation in embedded systems without opening embedded systems

The first form implies that ES providers design their system in accordance with open innovation. Thus, the ES provider needs to take a design effort enabling externals to participate. This form reflects Chesbrough's view on open innovation, putting the opening of the ES by the ES provider at the center. The main challenge for this form of OI is the corresponding opening of the system itself. The paradigm of open innovation, however, mainly refers to the opening of innovation processes.

Research on OI already offers some literature on OI revolving around technical systems. To allow users to express or to implement their own product needs, firms for instance offer 'open innovation toolkits' for their customers. With the help of these (often internet-based) toolkits, customers can autonomously and incrementally implement their solution without the direct involvement of the firm. Thus, the goal of these toolkits is to allow customers to create additional products or product variants which can be sold to a broader mass market (Reichwald and Piller 2006). In the computing sector, firms often offer integrated development environments (IDEs) which allow customers to write their own code and support the development process as a whole. Examples for such toolkits in the software development sector are e.g. the Eclipse IDE by the Eclipse foundation or Visual Studio by Microsoft. Regarding ES, toolkits would also facilitate open innovation. However, toolkits do not address the need for opening the ES itself. Rather, the product architecture of the ES must already be customizable to some degree to support the implementation of customer needs. This requires the ES firm to design their systems explicitly with the aim of allowing open innovation. This goes beyond open innovation in the sense, that it not only involves opening the innovation process. Rather, firms would design and open their underlying system in accordance with their open innovation strategy.

A field, where the product architecture is more congruent to open innovation, is the field of open source software. In contrast to open innovation, though, open source does not address the business model as a source for value creation and capture, but only focuses on value creation (Chesbrough, 2006). Thus, it rather describes general principles of sharing source code. Furthermore, the specific perspective of open source on source code does not offer a comprehensive system's perspective.

The second form, *OI in ES without opening ES*, does not presuppose the opening of the underlying ES. Therefore, it covers OI without the explicit endorsement by the ES provider. In contrast to the first form of OI in ES, it rather deals with more unexpected cases of OI driven by users. It thus falls in von Hippel's view on OI. An example for this form of OI can be seen in 'use-generative goods ('bien génératifs d'usage') as coined by (Brown 2013). The term denotes the notion of goods, whose purpose may be defined by the producer, but where the user employs the good in a different, unanticipated way.

Nonetheless of its more unexpected occurrence, the consideration of this form of OI allows to draw additional conclusions. For ES firms, this form of OI allows to learn from more disruptive, unexpected ways of using their systems. In addition, by comparing it with OI through opening ES, a clearer picture of the requirements for open innovation in

ES can be gained. Furthermore, it allows analyzing how firms react to open innovation and finding ways of benefitting from it.

In the context of this thesis, both of these forms of OI will be considered. However, the first form of OI (*OI in ES by opening ES*) will be the main focus, as the opening process required for that approach offers a broad potential to extend existing research on OI. This examination of 'OI in ES by opening ES' has an organizational and a technical dimension. The organizational dimension consists of exploring how the opening of innovation processes should be conducted. The technical dimension refers to designing and opening the underlying ES in accordance with open innovation.

Furthermore, *OI in ES by opening ES* can also be differentiated according to its scope. ES firms may carry out open innovation practices to enhance their product with additional applications. However, in this case the main purpose of the ES is still defined by the ES provider. Besides this form of open innovation, there are an increasing number of ES platforms emerging, e.g. Arduino or Raspberry PI, which do not possess a designated purpose. Rather, the purpose of these ES platforms is defined by the user. Thus, open innovation in ES can vary broadly in scope, ranging from minor additions by externals to externals determining the designation of the ES itself. Depending on the scope of open innovation, different challenges arise. In the later empirical part, this thesis will consider systems with different degrees of opening ES.

The second form of openness (*OI without opening ES*) will also be incorporated in this thesis. However, from a firms' perspective, this form does not presume any opening by the ES provider. Thus, the focus of the examination is less on the firm's activities, but more on the different ways users are extending a system, which has not been opened for OI. For ES firms, this allows to gain additional insights how OI in ES takes place.

4 Openness

In the last chapter, it was shown, that open innovation in ES often involves opening the underlying ES as well. By opening the underlying technical system, externals would not only be able to communicate their ideas, but they would be able to implement their ideas themselves. This does not imply that opening a system is always required for open innovation to take place, as a system may already be extensible without explicit opening by the ES provider. However, opening an ES allows the ES provider to determine explicitly which parts of the system should be extensible. Whereas the last chapter just emphasized the need for openness of ES for OI, this chapter aims to elaborate the notion of openness in detail.

This chapter aims to clarify the concept of openness and to present literature on openness. First of all, the use and meaning of the concept of openness is explained. Following in section 4.2, openness of computer systems will be discussed. More specifically, section 4.3 discusses openness in ES and potential constraints. This discussion especially shows how the technical characteristics of ES limit openness. However, discussing technical constraints does not yet touch on how ES can and should be opened from an open innovation perspective. To provide a theoretical foundation for these questions, two different theoretical perspectives will be presented.

First of all, in section 4.4, literature on platforms will be used to shed light on potential openness strategies. The literature on platforms already provides insights how open innovation takes place in technical settings. With platforms allowing externals to built on them with complementary solutions, they represent technical systems where OI is already realized to a certain degree. At the same time, when opening an ES for open innovation, the objective by ES providers is to partly turn the ES into a platform to spur complementary innovation. However, the platform perspective takes a general nature and does not consider specific technical characteristics such as in the ES domain.

This gap is addressed by section 4.5, which builds on literature on modularity to provide a framework to analyze openness in ES from a technical point of view. Existing theory on modularity helps to explore how ES must be designed to realize openness. As it has been mentioned before, openness usually takes place partially, with some parts of the system being opened whereas other parts remain closed. Modularity theory helps to describe those systems and explains how these systems can be structured. Thus, it will be used to analyze the design of ES in accordance with openness.

4.1 Definition of openness

Openness as a system's attribute has been discussed in an array of research disciplines ranging from biology or physics (Von Bertalanffy 1950), economics (Grunberg 1978; Loasby 2003), systems theory, organization design and strategy (Garud and Kumaraswamy 1993; Lecocq and Demil 2006; Pondy and Mitroff 1979) and management to computer science (Halsall 1996).

In physics, openness of a system means that material can both be imported or exported from a system implying a change of components of a system, whereas closed systems do not allow this change of material (Von Bertalanffy 1950). This rather simple definition already exhibits a foundational characteristic of open systems, namely the possibility of an exchange of certain parts or components.

Drawing from physics, kinetics and thermodynamics, the concept of open systems has become a core concept in systems theory (Von Bertalanffy 1968). The concept of a system itself has been used throughout various science fields, with system theory aiming to provide a general theory of systems valid across different fields of science. However, an open system can be described differently in a particular science, e.g. Bertalanffy (1993) lays out the general characteristics of open chemical systems and biology.

In electrical and computer science, the open systems concept has been firmly established. The "Technical Committee of Open Systems" which is part of the IEEE (Institute of Electrical and Electronics Engineering) offers a definition for open systems: "An open system provides capabilities that enable properly implemented applications to run on a variety of platforms from multiple vendors, interoperate with other system applications and present a consistent style of interaction with the user" (IEEE 1003.0)[1].

This definition of an open system by the IEEE extends the former definitions of open systems as they also mention certain actors (multiple vendors as well as users) which can interact with an open system. In contrast to the more general definitions of open systems, it also denotes a specific purpose of openness in a system. Openness here especially relates to integrate certain applications on platforms provided by different vendors. Another definition of open systems by the Unix X/Open consortium states that open systems rely on standards that are vendor-independent and commonly available. For technologies, openness refers to the notion easing of restrictions on the use, development and commercialization of a technology (Boudreau 2010; Shapiro and Varian 1999) . Eisenmann, Parker, & Van Alstyne (2008) also apply this view on openness also for technical platforms. For this dissertation, it will be built on this understanding of openness.

This understanding of openness also emphasizes the objectives of openness (allowing the use, development and commercialization), being in line with the goal of this dissertation, namely to explore openness for third-party innovation. Less restrictions regarding use, development and commercialization would stimulate third-party innovation and thus emphasizes the participation of externals. Furthermore, it implies, that openness represents a multidimensional concept, which can exhibit different degrees of openness.

---

[1] See https://standards.ieee.org/findstds/standard/1003.0-1995.html

The next section further operationalizes openness by discussing how a certain degree of openness is chosen.

Degree of openness

The decision for a particular degree of openness is associated with the risks and potentials of openness. Opening the innovation process already gives rise to a number of risks, such as a lack of market and technological knowledge, difficulties of protecting intellectual property, as well as threats arising from competitors due to market entries or imitation. Thus, for management, the degree of openness for innovation constitute a key strategic decision (Drechsler and Natter 2012). Laursen & Salter (2006) suggest that there is an optimal degree of openness, after which further increasing openness leads to decreasing returns.

As open innovation for embedded systems also entails opening the underlying ES itself, the necessity of choosing the optimal degree of openness is even more crucial. On the one hand, the opening of the underlying ES has to be done in accordance with the goals of open innovation. On the other hand, the technical dimension of ES adds further complexity. Some of the risks associated with the opening of the innovation process are amplified with the corresponding opening of the ES. Risks arising from the exposure of the system regarding intellectual property protection and the protection from imitation are further exacerbated in these settings. With the opening of ES, externals would get a higher level of access to the individual components the system. According to Henkel (2006), the degree of openness varies with the need for collaborative development with externals, with firms requiring more external development support also releasing a larger share of their code to externals.

Managers therefore do not only need to decide to what degree innovation processes will be opened, but they also need to consider which parts of their ES can be disclosed without taking too high risks. They must decide which parts of their system constitute strategic components, which should not be disclosed, and which parts can be opened without hazarding their own business.

To evaluate the degree of openness of an ES, first of all, it needs to be clarified, how the degree of openness is embodied in a system and what approaches towards openness firms use. A theoretical perspective from management research which helps to answer what parts of a system can be opened is the Resource-Based View (RBV). The RBV aims to explain how firms achieve sustainable competitive advantage by the application of certain resources a firm possesses (Armstrong and Shimizu 2007; Barney 1991; Wernerfelt 1984). It assumes that the strategic resources of firms are quite heterogeneous and at the same time not completely mobile and therefore not easily transferable across firms. Due to this not-perfect mobility of strategic resources firms possess, the heterogeneity between firms can prevail through long time periods (Barney 1991).

The resource-based view could be used to decide which resources can be opened and which should remain closed. Although the RBV originated from management literature, it can also serve as a framework to examine tangible systems like ES. In the context of ES, the RBV allows viewing the components of a system as distinct resources, which contribute to the competitive advantage of the system. For that purpose, the notion of resources needs to be elaborated.

The term resource itself denotes a rather broad spectrum of both intangible and tangible assets a company possesses. Wade & Hulland (2004) list several examples of resources mentioned in the literature, e.g. competences, skills, strategic assets, assets and stocks. In addition, they provide a definition of resources, which encompasses "*assets and capabilities that are available and useful in detecting and responding to market opportunities and threats*". Assets in this regard can either be tangible or intangible and be inputs or outputs of a process (Wade and Hulland 2004). Concerning ES, such tangible resources are for instance hardware assets or network infrastructure, whereas examples for intangible assets are software patents or vendor relationships (Wade and Hulland 2004).

To identify strategic resources, which help to achieve competitive advantage, the question arises, how these resources can be identified. According to Barney (1991), firm resources have four attributes determining whether they cause sustained competitive advantage, which have been summarized in the VRIO framework:

- **Valuable:** a valuable resource either allows firms to gain from opportunities or to neutralize threats

- **Rare**: resources are rare, when they are not possessed by many different firms, as in that case, the resource itself would not be a source of competitive advantage

- **Imitable**: a resource can be imitated for instance by duplication or substitution; a resource providing a competitive advantage must not be imitated without cost disadvantages by other parties

- **need organizational support:** besides being valuable, rare and difficult to imitate, to gain from such resources involves the organization being able to exploit the potential of its resources; this also refers to complementary resources required to tap the potential of a firm's valuable resources

At a later stage, Barney (1995) updated the original framework, referring to it as the VRIN framework, with the letter N referring to the non-substitutability of an asset. This framework supports ES firms facing the decision which firm's resources they should open and which should remain closed. Thus, a certain degree of openness can be implemented on a per-resource level.

However, the RBV offers a very general view, which does not specifically address ES and their specific kinds of resources. To operationalize which mechanisms can be used to implement a certain degree of openness, the specific kinds of resources in the context of ES need to be considered. Schlagwein, Schoder, & Fischbach (2010) address this issue in a study of mobile platforms by classifying open information resources according to different degrees of openness. An information resource refers to information both economically relevant as well as repeatedly available. These open information resources can be classified along two dimensions: *access to resource* and *control of resource*. The access dimension expresses the parties having access to a particular information resource and has three different values: *open*, *group* and *exclusive*. Control denotes the ability of firms to control who has access to the information resource. The values of the control dimension are *internal*, *shared*, and *external*. Figure 3 shows the dimensions and the different types of openness at the intersections of both dimensions.

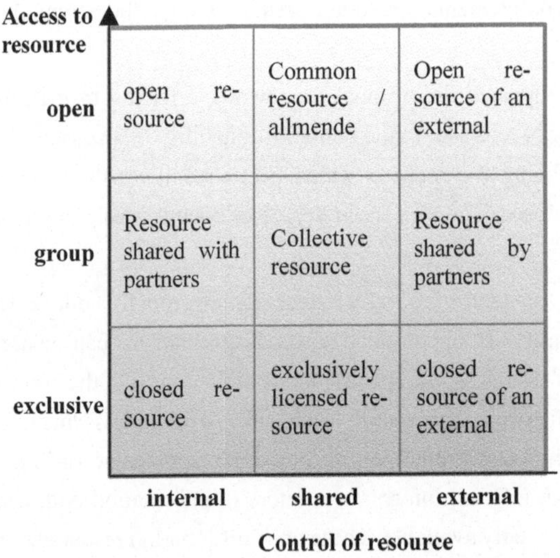

Access to
resource

	internal	shared	external
open	open re-source	Common resource / allmende	Open re-source of an external
group	Resource shared with partners	Collective resource	Resource shared by partners
exclusive	closed re-source	exclusively licensed re-source	closed re-source of an external

internal   shared   external

Control of resource

Figure 3   Open resources: Access and control according to Schlagwein, Schoder, & Fischbach (2010)

The framework of information resources suggested by Schlagwein et al. (2010) espe-cially emphasizes the resources which are part of the product itself. Thus, it helps to classify the resources of a system, which constitute the different components of a system. Both decisions regarding openness (granting access to a resource or giving up control of a resource) can be made by considering the VRIO status of these resources.

4.2   Openness in computer systems

In the field of computer systems, openness has been a widely researched notion. Espe-cially with the emergence of general-purpose computer systems like personal computers, openness for third-party applications became one of the design goals of computer sys-tems. To allow for such extensions by externals, computer systems have been specifically designed to accommodate for such extensions. Although embedded systems are not an example for such general-purpose-systems, an examination of these systems allows to understand how systems are designed for openness.

To provide an operationalization where openness in a computer system can occur, it will be drawn on the layer model of computer systems. Openness can be classified according to these layers, with openness on the software layer comprising of openness on the ap-plication as well as on the operating system (OS) layer. Figure 4 depicts openness on these different layers.

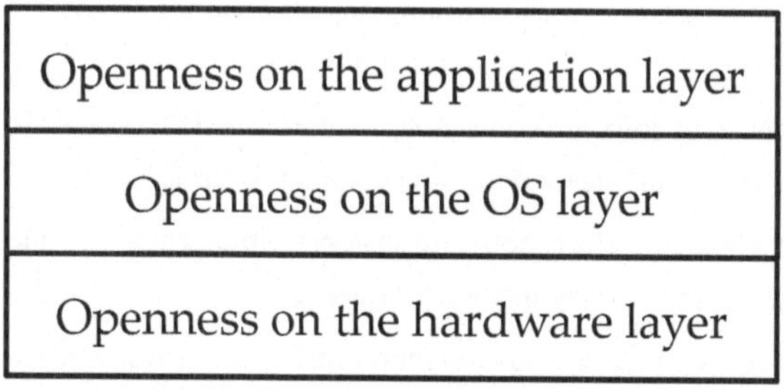

| Openness on the application layer |
| Openness on the OS layer |
| Openness on the hardware layer |

Figure 4   Openness on different layers of computer systems

Although, each of these three layers can be opened, extending the system on the hard-ware layer holds additional challenges. Due to its intangible character, software can be more easily changed and modified than physical goods. Thus, openness for software components is comparably cheap in contrast to changing hardware components. The in-tangibility of software has facilitated openness, as it allows the distributed development by externals without the requirement of special equipment or machinery for develop-ment.

4.2.1   Openness on the software layer

According to Buckley et al. (2005), software can be classified as open when it is explic-itly built to allow for extensions. For instance, a system can offer an extension point allowing externals to provide plug-ins to a system. Klatt (2008) defines an extension point as "a well-defined interface between the extension and the extended system or other extension. One way to provide this extension points is by offering open application pro-gramming interfaces (APIs). Often, embedded systems do not offer open APIs, as they traditionally have been designed and implemented solely by the ES provider. In prac-tices, examples of ES which often do not provide an open API are for instance certain vehicle functions as customizing e.g. engine functionality would pose risks in terms of safety and security (Gunter and Alur 2003). Although providing APIs to externals is a very common approach regarding openness, there are other mechanisms as well. Alspaugh, Asuncion, & Scacchi (2009) describe further elements determining the open-ness of a software architecture:

- Software source code components: The presence of certain programs, libraries etc. which can be used by externals

- Executable components: binary programs which can (may not) be open for access, review and modification

- Software connectors: the presence of software connectors such as CORBA, MS .NET etc. provide a standardized way of communication through common interfaces

- Configured system or sub-system architecture: software systems, which could include subcomponents with different licenses affecting the overall license

Jansen, Brinkkemper, Hunink, & Demir (2008) also mention different software extension mechanisms, namely component calls, service calls, source code inclusion and shared data objects. Specific for the operating systems layer, Alexandrov et al. (1997) mention specific extension mechanisms, i.e. changing the operating system itself, modifying device drivers, installing a network server, adding user-level plugins or making changes to them, application specific modifications and intercept system calls.

Open source

The notion of open source describes the practice of distributing source code of software and the right to modify the software (Fosfuri, Giarratana, and Luzzi 2008; Raymond 1999; Vonkrogh and Spaeth 2007; West and Gallagher 2006b). This is ensured by putting source code under a license, which grants these rights to every user – a license called General Public License (http://www.gnu.org/licenses/gpl.html). It gained rapid traction with popular examples of large open source projects such as the Linux operating system, the Apache web server or the PERL programming language.

Literature on open source itself does not assume that it takes place in a corporate setting, but rather primarily focuses on the free distribution and changeability of source code comprising different kinds of actors without focusing on commercialization of the source code. Although the principles of open source are aimed to provide free access to source code without relying on proprietary mechanisms, firms have begun to implement open source strategies, i.e. incorporating open source code in their overall code base, but still rely on proprietary source for other parts of their code base. Some firms are even participating in "revealing" some parts of their code as open source (Henkel 2006; von Hippel and von Krogh 2006). For firms, investing in open source software can be beneficial when their own commercial product profits from the open source code. These benefits arise either due to nesting open source code within their own product or due to complementarities between the firm's own proprietary code and the open source code (Fosfuri, Giarratana, and Luzzi 2008; Haruvy, Sethi, and Zhou 2008). An open source strategy can already be seen as an example for open innovation, as firms are taking ideas from outside and incorporate them in their own product. In addition to incorporating open source code, firms are often revealing parts of their own code to the general public and thus making it open source (von Hippel and von Krogh 2006). In the context of ES, Henkel (2006) describes such practices for embedded Linux. In a quantitative study with firms in the field of ES, he found out, that many of these firms are contributing to embedded Linux. They do this on a selective basis, in order to protect intellectual property, a strategy Henkel (2006) coined as 'selective revealing'. By releasing some of their source code as open source, they aim to spur informal development collaboration with outsiders (Feller and Fitzgerald 2002; Henkel 2006). From the example of firms contributing to open source, it can be inferred, that firms can determine openness to a degree, which protects their commercial interests. Henkel (2006) along this line found out that firms decide for different degrees of openness in dependence with their need of collaborating with externals.

For embedded systems, this can be seen as one form of opening embedded systems to enable open innovation, but besides open source, firms can also employ other openness mechanisms. Open source in contrast to open systems mainly focuses on user rights, enabling shared development and collaboration (West and Gallagher 2006b).

4.2.2 Openness on the hardware layer

Openness in the field of hardware goods has been mainly approached in the literature by analyzing whether open source principles can be transferred to non-software domains, e.g. by Abdelkafi, Blecker, & Raasch (2009), who evaluate the difference between physical products and software which influence the applicability of open source principles. The use of open source principles in the context of hardware has been captured by different terms: open hardware, open source hardware and open design. The use of these terms is not always consistent in the literature. Therefore, the next paragraphs explain the different uses of these terms in the literature.

According to Hansen & Howard (2013), the literature basically offers two different terms describing open source in the hardware context: open design as well as open source hardware. Furthermore, the term 'open source hardware' is also often used interchangeably with 'open hardware'.

Open design, however, also has a different connotation: It means the development of tangible products in accordance to open source principles (Raasch and Herstatt 2011;

Vallance, Kiani, and Nayfeh 2001). However, it does not only refer to computing hardware, but includes all kinds of tangible products. According to Raasch & Herstatt (2011), open design projects have for instance been taken place in products ranging from beverages or furniture to automotive products or robots. Although open design is based on open source principles, most open design products are bundles of both open and proprietary components, representing different degrees of openness (Raasch and Herstatt 2011).

A recent definition of open source hardware stems from the open hardware community (http://freedomdefined.org/Definition): "Open source hardware is hardware whose design is made publicly available so that anyone can study, modify, distribute, make, and sell the design or hardware based on that design." Popular examples of open source hardware are e.g. the Arduino programmable micro-controller (Mellis and Buechley 2012), open-source 3d printers (RepRap) or the Openmoko phone. Here, open hardware here is used in the broader sense, also encompassing non-computing products.

Due to the tangible aspects of hardware, transferring open source principles to hardware holds specific challenges. Whereas the sharing of construction plans for hardware components can be done via the internet, the production process requires resources like factories and special machine equipment.

Besides implementing open source principles, another characteristic for openness in hardware is that the products are often modular, or designed with the intent of being modular. However, Raasch et al. (2009) also come up with an example of a product ("Free Beer") which is not modular, but due to the low level of complexity, collaborative and distributed task fulfillment is facilitated.

To extend the scope of openness towards hardware, Balka, Raasch, & Herstatt (2009) extend the model of software openness suggested by West & O'Mahony (2008) which is based on the two aspects of transparency and accessibility. They suggested a third factor, replicability in order to account for hardware aspects. Replicability refers to the availability of hardware components and the possibility of self-assembly.

Although the phenomenon of openness in hardware is increasing rapidly in popularity, the literature is still rather scarce. This implies that for exploring openness in embedded systems, the existing body of knowledge does not provide extensive answers. Another literature stream which partly deals with hardware aspects is the literature on platforms which will be discussed in Chapter 4.4. However, platforms do not only consider hardware platforms, as there also could be pure software platforms.

4.3 Openness of ES

It has been argued that the openness of ES is crucial for conducting open innovation in embedded systems. For understanding OI in ES, there are thus two facets of openness: (1) the opening of the innovation processes (open innovation), which will be referred to as organizational openness and (2) the technical opening of the ES itself.

Although there has already been a lot of literature on organizational openness for open innovation, the context of embedded systems raises additional challenges. Furthermore, the technical openness opening of ES for open innovation has only been marginally considered in the literature. This chapter therefore will consider organizational openness as well as technical openness.

4.3.1 Organizational openness of ES

In this section, organizational openness associated with the opening of ES for open innovation will be discussed. Organizing for openness still represents a challenge to open innovation for which the literature did not provide a comprehensive model so far (Giannopoulou, Yström, and Ollila 2011). One aspect which is challenging for firms implementing open innovation is the required organizational structure, as firms are often not attuned to collaboration with a wide variety of actors (Elmquist, Fredberg, and Ollila 2009). Firms also need to have the ability to identify external innovation and have the absorptive capacity to incorporate external innovations. Furthermore, firms need to be willing to accept external innovations by overcoming internal resistance like the "not invented here" syndrome (Laursen and Salter 2006; West and Gallagher 2006a). According to West et al. (2006), it is quite likely, that open innovation requires internal reorganization in order to build the internal organizational capacities to integrate external knowledge, namely by complementary internal networks. For managers, adopting an open strategy requires the establishing of corresponding organizational structures and processes (Giannopoulou, Yström, and Ollila 2011). Drechsler & Natter (2012) identified a number of factors preventing the decision for openness: knowledge gaps which concerning the market and technologies, the difficulty to protect intellectual property and threats from competitor such as market entries and imitation.

Another factor for the organization results from the fact, that opening ES would evoke additional challenges due to the management of ecosystems emerging from the opening. According to Baldwin (2012), the management of distributed innovation in ecosystems, comprising of a variety of corporations, individuals and communities whose connection is based on an underlying technical system, constitutes a key challenge towards organizational design. In particular the question how the diverse actors in such an ecosystem can be integrated needs to be answered (Baldwin, 2012). Due to the role of the technical system as an underlying base in ecosystems, an understanding of the technical characteristics of the system is required to inform organization design (Baldwin, 2012).

Regarding open innovation in ES, this means that the organizational openness needs to be informed by the underlying technical system at place. Therefore, the influence of the technical characteristic on organizational openness needs to be clarified. In line with Baldwin (2012), this still represents a challenge which needs to be answered by the literature. In the context of this thesis, this represents one of the research gaps this thesis aims to answer. The next section will consider potential technical challenges for the opening of ES.

4.3.2   Technical openness of ES

In chapter II.2., the characteristics of embedded systems have been expounded. Some of these characteristics are crucial for the proper functioning of the ES and influence the design of ES. These factors are: dependability, resource and cost efficiency, sensors and actuators, real-time constraints, reactive systems, hybrid systems, dedicated user interfaces as well as being dedicated towards specific applications. To differentiate between the openness of general-purpose computing systems and openness of ES, the impact of these factors needs to be considered. Some of these individual aspects may have specific consequences for ES design and thus for potential openness whereas some may not affect openness. This section therefore aims to explain each of these characteristics in more detail and how they affect ES openness.

Dependability

The characteristic of dependability itself captures a sub-set of characteristics which are reliability, maintainability, availability, safety and security The next paragraphs give a short description of these characteristics (Marwedel 2011).:

(1) Reliability: Reliability captures the probability of a system running without failures.

(2) Maintainability: Maintainability denotes the probability of being able to repair a failing system in a certain time frame.

(3) Availability: Availability results from reliability and maintainability and refers to the probability that the system is available.

(4) Safety: Safety refers to the property of a system, that it will not cause any harm.

(5) Security: Security refers to the property of protecting confidential data and to the guarantee of authentic communication.

Different types of ES need to fulfill these characteristics to varying degrees. Whereas for some ES, all of these aspects are highly critical (e.g. automotive ES, production machinery), other ES are less critical in that regard (e.g. consumer electronics). With increasing criticality of these characteristics, opening ES is also constrained. Thus, they require specific approaches towards ensuring these constraints.

Resource and Cost Efficiency

ES are traditionally taking a subordinate role in a larger product or environment, and are subject to restrictive cost and resource savings. The design and the selection of components for ES thus are thus constrained by these aspects. Therefore, ES would often not have the capabilities to support additional applications which are not yet known during design time (Gunter and Alur 2003). An industry, where this is particularly visible, is the automotive industry, where the costs of individual ES components is crucial for competitiveness. For systems whose requirements are known at design time, this is a valid approach. However, such a strict resource and cost efficiency regime would inhibit openness where additional requirements would be implemented after the production of the ES. As a consequence, opening ES may require using components which have additional capabilities to enable openness.

Even though openness may lead to less efficient ES and may lead to higher prices, its advantages often outweigh the drawbacks. As long as the consumer perceives the extra utility of openness higher, reduced efficiency can be accepted. An example is the reduced battery life of smart phones in contrast to older mobile phones. Here, power consumption has increased due to the variety of new applications enabled through additional hardware capabilities.

Sensors and actuators

A particular feature of ES is the presence of sensors and actuators allowing interaction with the environment. Furthermore, their presence allow to realize different kinds of applications not offered by standard PCs. Opening ES can also entail the attachment and implementation of additional sensors and actuators. By changing the hardware base, externals would be able to broaden the range of use cases for ES. However, the presence of actuators also has consequences regarding dependability and safety of a system, as the actuators are affecting the environment of a system and therefore can potentially be hazardous (Johannessen, Törner, and Torin 2004). Thus, this also affects potential openness, as it requires to set up rules concerning openness for additional actuators, i.e. requiring coordination of critical hardware abstraction applications concerning access (Eklund and Bosch 2012). Eklund & Bosch (2012) suggest categorizing applications, which use actuators into three categories with different levels of access to the hardware abstraction:

- Applications with critical functionality

- Certified applications

- Any application

To increase flexibility for applications and at the same time guaranteeing dependability requirements, one solution would be to introduce different usage modes. Examples for rules governing such usage modes would be that applications can only get data from hardware with required safety integrity levels or that open applications cannot access services from critical applications (Eklund and Bosch 2012). In summary, ES openness regarding sensors and actuators requires certain coordination and design decisions to ensure safety.

Real-time constraints

The implications of real-time constraints on ES openness are similar to the implications of dependability characteristics. When those constraints are present, their abidance is critical to the proper functioning of the ES. Thus, opening ES regarding RT constraints has certain design implications: On the one hand, it needs to be ensured, that the ES observes the RT-constraints. On the other hand, the ES needs to provide capabilities to accommodate additional applications without competing for scarce resources. Consequently, the presence of RT constraints does not necessarily hinder openness but influences the design for openness.

Reactive systems

The characteristic of being a reactive system especially refers to the fact, that ES respond to events triggered by the environment. The ES registers these events by its sensors. For ES openness, this behavior does not necessarily involve additional challenges, as long as openness does not jeopardize the system's behavior. Reactive systems are also often subject to RT-constraints, whose implications have been stated above. However, the characteristic of being 'reactive' to input from the environment can also be found in general-purpose systems.

Hybrid systems

The characteristic of being a hybrid system refers to the fact that ES consist of analog and digital parts. Although ES often have to process analog signals, especially when registering signals form the environment, further processing in ES is usually done in a digital form, requiring an analog signal to be converted into a digital signal. Processing digital signals are usually easier to process, as the processing components are built to work with digital signals. In terms of opening ES, this characteristic of ES does not necessarily have an influence.

Dedicated user interface

The significance of dedicated user interface is more and more decreasing, as more and more ES offer the possibility to be managed or controlled by external devices like tablets or smart phones. The example of ES in smart homes already indicates this trend. Therefore, this characteristic of ES would rather loose importance concerning openness.

Dedicated towards a specific application

Traditionally, embedded systems have a clearly specified role, which leaves little room for customizations or additional use cases. This has a clear impact on the design of the ES itself, especially regarding the capabilities an ES offer. This characteristic directly contradicts the notion of opening ES, as openness is implemented to allow for unforeseen requirements and thus new applications for a given system. Openness in ES rather represents a move towards ES, which are less specific regarding their future applications. Consequently, opening ES represents a move towards more general-purpose systems. This also implies that ES need to be designed differently, in order to account for these additional requirements.

Conclusively, this section has shown the implications of the specific characteristics of ES concerning openness. Whereas some of the characteristics do not affect openness, other factors have a large impact on the design for openness. In particular, ES firms need to align their openness decisions with the constraints ES face, such as safety and security or real-time requirements. The potential impact of these characteristics is depicted in table 3. However, the question remains how firms should consider these factors in the design of open ES and regarding the open innovation process. These questions will later be tackled in the empirical part.

Furthermore, an operationalization of openness for the later empirical analysis is still missing. The next section thus will further elaborate the notion of openness from a platforms literature perspective.

Table 3   Impact of technical factors of ES on openness

Factor	Potential impact on openness on ES
Dependability	Openness is constrained due to dependability requirements, especially safety considerations
Efficiency	The perceived utility of openness must be higher than the reduction in efficiency
Sensors and actuators	Openness to sensor or actuators may imply safety risks, which can be avoided by giving restricted access
Real-time constraints	RT-constraints constitute a constraint which cannot be violated
Reactive systems	No traceable influence on openness
Hybrid systems	No traceable influence on openness
Dedicated user interface	This characteristic does not need to be uphold when opening ES
Dedicated towards a specific application	This characteristics describes how traditional ES are designed, however openness aims to extend use cases, thus weakening the relevance of this characteristic

4.4   Openness from a platforms perspective

4.4.1   Platforms

Exploring openness in settings such as embedded systems can benefit by drawing to research fields where similar phenomena have already been discussed, such as openness of platforms. Research on platforms does not specifically deal with embedded systems, but nonetheless offers many insights for this thesis. Existing research of platforms is also of interest, because it also deals with the economic factors underlying decisions towards openness. This chapter consists of the following parts: first of all, the term platform will be discussed and to what extent research on platform openness is useful for the specific field of embedded systems.

A platform can be conceptualized as a "technical architecture that allows compatible complements to use it" (Gawer 2009) which is normally governed by a platform leader who provides access to the platform for other parties to develop complementary goods and services (Eisenmann et al. 2008; Mikkola and Skjøtt-Larsen 2006; Parker and Van Alstyne 2005). Therefore, general-purpose computer systems can be conceptualized as platforms, as they constitute a modular architecture consisting of hardware and software parts, for which additional software can be developed. ES, as it has been shown in II.2, depart from this definition as they are usually designated towards a specific application. However, with the opening of ES for open innovation and thus, with the broadening of use cases, ES are becoming platforms to some degree. Therefore, due to this openness for complementary applications, research on platforms also offers valuable insights for ES. Similarly, the computer industry also started with proprietary platforms, where a whole computer system consisting of hardware and software layers was controlled by a single manufacturer. Later on, the dominance of proprietary platforms has been challenged by the emergence of the hardware-independent operating systems Windows and Linux (West 2003). With ES moving into the direction of platforms, similar developments could be expected for ES as well.

4.4.2 Openness of platforms

Openness in platform itself has been defined by Eisenmann et al. (2008) as the degree of restrictions placed on use, development and commercialization of a platform. Thus, this definition resembles the definition of openness of technologies introduced in 4.1. Restrictions need not necessarily be discriminatory and deny access to a platform for a particular group of users, but can also be applied to externals in general, such as the requirement to conform to technical standards or the demand to pay license fees (Eisenmann et al. 2008). Parker & Van Alstyne (2012) offer a more simplistic definition of platform openness. According to them, platform openness is the "degree to which sponsor firms share platform technologies with third-party developers", thus focusing more on the target group of openness, namely third-party developers.

Openness of platforms can be differentiated in two basic types: vertical openness and horizontal openness. A platform is vertically opened, when externals can provide either complementary products or services on top of the platform. The second form of platform openness, horizontal openness, entails opening a platform for competitors or to incorporate additional platform sponsors (Eisenmann et al. 2008; Hilkert, Benlian, and Hess 2011). For this dissertation especially the first type of platform openness, vertical openness, is relevant, as the general theme of this dissertation is to allow open innovation by externals to develop complementary assets.

To achieve this aim, Boudreau (2010) suggests two distinct approaches: granting access to a platform to enable complementary development by third parties, and giving up control over the platform or parts of the platform. Although these constitute two separate approaches, they often take place at the same time. When firms completely devolve control, access to the platform cannot be restricted anymore. Examples for such cases can be found in the smart phone industry, where key platform technologies have been made public standards. For instance, the Android operating system is used by a variety of different smart phone producers. In contrast, Apple with its iPhone operating system iOS, holds tighter control of its platform, but still attracted a vast community of developers accessing the system and building complementary applications (Boudreau 2010).

Regardless of the chosen approach, when opening a platform, firms have to reconcile two contradictory goals: appropriability and adoption. Appropriability refers to the need to realize economic benefits with the platform whereas adoption refers to the goal of broadening the user base using the platform (West 2003). Appropriating value from a technology requires firms to appropriate value from their intellectual property rights (IPR) regime – this can result from patents, thus de jure protection or from de facto protection mechanisms, e.g. through tacit knowledge or trade secrets (Teece 1986). Although Teece (1986) refers to technologies, a platform constitutes a specific form of technological innovations studied by him (West 2003). Besides appropriability, Teece (1986) suggests two other building blocks which facilitate profiting from innovation: *complementary assets* and the *dominant design* paradigm.

For many innovations, the existence of complementary assets is crucial. Such an asset can be for instance a marketing channel used to dissipate information about an innovation. When the innovation is part of a platform or a system, it is usually dependent on other parts of the system, e.g. in computer platforms, hardware innovations are dependent on specialized software innovations or an operating system which runs on the particular hardware (Teece 1986). A primary mechanism to allow for complementary assets in computer platforms is to provide APIs, which basically determine how complementary software assets need to communicate to a particular platform (West and Dedrick 2000).

Dominant designs are another mechanism for the emergence of innovations in the context of platforms. Before a dominant design evolves in a market, several designs are competing with each other without a predominant design which covers all user needs.

After some time, a dominant design evolves as a particular promising design which fulfills the bulk of user needs. Examples of dominant designs are the Model T Ford, or the IBM 360. With the emergence of a dominant design, competition is rather based on the price than on the design (Teece 1986).

The goal of increasing adoption of a platform is to gain network effects and increase the variety of applications for the platform which would attract more users to the platform (Boudreau 2011). Besides network effects, other benefits of opening platforms are to mitigate the risks for users to be locked-in and to animate the development of differentiated goods (Eisenmann et al. 2008), the refinement of individual components, the development of complementary goods, the removal of bugs and "the accumulation of quality and cost" (Boudreau 2008). Opening platforms for the development of complementary applications can be seen as an example of open innovation, when the ES firms are able to appropriate some of the returns associated with the complementary applications. Complementary applications can be sold by firms themselves or provided by external actors, increasing the value of a product (Bogers and West 2012; Teece 1986). To enable complementary development, outsiders need to get access to the core platform, but the platform owner does not need to give up control of the platform (Boudreau 2008). This reflects two different consequences when opening a platform, namely providing access to the platform in order to enable complementary innovation, and giving up some control (Boudreau 2010). In his paper, Boudreau (2010) found out by studying 26 handheld computing systems that granting more access on the platform to hardware developers accelerated development of new handheld devices by a fivefold rate. This was dependent on the degree of access and the policy by which this has been implemented. However, according to Boudreau (2010), a unified concept of openness could not be found, as a lot of different technical and contractual procedures have been applied to realize a variety of different policies by the platform owners.

The smart phone sector with its focus on third-party apps offers an insightful research object for studies focusing on platform openness. For instance, Anvaari & Jansen (2010) examine different openness strategies of five different mobile architectures in terms of its success to spur ecosystem growth. Another study by Hilkert et al. (2011) explores the role of software platform openness for application development in the smart phone sector. In this paper, they focused on the developer's view of perceived platform openness. The rapid change which has been occurring in the smart phone sector due to technological change has been analyzed by Basole & Karla (2011).

Due to the inherent openness of platforms for complementary goods and services, platforms are already exhibiting patterns of open innovation. For computing platforms, firms usually have a third-party development strategy to foster the development of complementary assets. Elements of such strategies are for instance "standard-form licensing contracts, development tools, documentation, and support in marketing and distribution" (Boudreau 2011). By supporting these external developers, which can be firms or merely external developers, a platform provider aims to build an ecosystem around his platform. In the software industry, these ecosystems are quite common, with popular examples in the B2C sector e.g. Apple with its App Store, Google with its Android marketplace or Microsoft with its Windows phone market place (Burkard, Widjaja, and Buxmann 2012). By organizing these ecosystems around a "marketplace", platform providers also retain control of their platform, as they can determine barriers of entry. Other examples from the B2B sector are salesforce.com (AppExchange), SugarCRM (SugarExchange) (Burkard, Widjaja, and Buxmann 2012). These ecosystems have a variety of advantages for the platform provider, among them the larger amount of functionality which can be developed by the ecosystem, or the fulfillment of a variety of different user needs and therefore generating more value for the customers (Bosch 2009). Firms being in a central position to exercise control in an ecosystem are described as platform leaders (Gawer and Cusumano 2002) or ecosystem orchestrators (Hinterhuber 2002). Platform providers often also absorb the innovations created in their ecosystem, e.g. Facebook copied diverse features from developers such as Snapchat, Foursquare or Groupon, or Microsoft, which adopted features ranging from disk defragmentation, encryption to web browsing (Parker, Alstyne, and Van Alstyne 2010).

4.4.3 Implications on ES openness

The literature on platforms explored in this section offers valuable insights for openness in ES. First of all, it elaborates the theme of partial openness and also provides insights about the underlying economics behind opening a platform. In terms of openness, the common challenge for platform providers is to find a corresponding degree of openness which allows them to benefit by external innovation without risking loosing too much of their intellectual property or allow imitation by competitors.

As embedded systems which are opened are an example of platforms, the economic underpinnings of platforms can also be applied to embedded systems. Therefore, the platform literature offers an approximation towards openness in ES. However, to tackle the specific challenges of ES, the platform literature offers a too general perspective. It does not provide a framework which can be used for the design of ES according to openness considerations. Furthermore, the specific technical challenges of opening ES are not addressed in the platforms literature. To complement the platform perspective, an additional perspective is needed which allows to explain how varying degrees of openness can be implemented.

On a technical level, realizing the desired level of openness entails opening certain parts of the system while keeping other parts closed. Thus, the opening of ES is realized on the level of individual modules. The next sections aim to introduce modularity theory, which can be used to tackle these challenges.

4.5 Openness from a modularity perspective

Embedded systems, which are traditionally designed for designated use cases, often may not exhibit an architecture allowing to open the ES to the desired degree. Therefore, one of the aims of this thesis is to answer how systems must be designed from an openness perspective. To achieve this research aim, modularity theory offers a valuable perspective as it describes how systems are partitioned into modules and how they interact with each other. In the present chapter, the foundations of modularity are described and how openness can be accomplished by applying the mechanisms of modular design.

4.5.1 Modularity

The notion of modularity applies to systems in general and refers to the degree to which the components of a system can be partitioned into separate modules and be recombined. In modular systems, interdependencies between different units are encapsulated in modules, whereas the degree of coupling between modules is minimized. The different modules thereby communicate through standardized interfaces (S. K. Ethiraj, Levinthal, and Roy 2008; Langlois 2002; Schilling 2000). Modularity therefore is a strategy to manage complexity (Langlois 2002). The concept of modularity builds on already established concepts like 'near-decomposability' and 'loose coupling' (Campagnolo and Camuffo 2009). Near-decomposability according to Simon (1962) describes systems whose subsystem's short-run behavior is almost independent of the short-run behavior of other subsystems. In contrast, components in decomposable systems are more dependent on other components in a specific subassembly (Langlois 2002).

Loose coupling of a system according to Weick (1967) refers to "a situation in which elements are responsive, but retain evidence of separateness and identity". Both of these concepts focus on the independence of sub-components of a system. Due to the reduced interdependencies between different components of a system, individual components can be more easily mix-and-matched. By having a weak level of coupling between modules, a module can be developed or changed without affecting others and without intense communication across modules (Baldwin and von Hippel 2011). Another advantage of modularity is, that it augments the number of possible configurations which can be created by a given set of input, therefore exhibiting a higher 'option value (Clark and Baldwin 2000; Schilling 2000). In product design, modularity at first was brought forward as a product design strategy with the goal of defining standardized interfaces for components. Gradually, modularity has been used in the fields of strategic management and industrial economics for the analysis of organizational designs, inter-firm relationships and knowledge dynamics (Brusoni and Prencipe 2001).

According to Ulrich & Eppinger (2000), modular designs are especially advantageous when the focus is on flexibility and rapid innovation rather than overall performance. In terms of innovation, modularity is especially valuable in systems focusing on incremental and modular innovation (S. K. Ethiraj, Levinthal, and Roy 2008). There are two mechanisms, by which product innovation is accelerated, autonomous innovation (innovation within a module) and modular innovation (innovation through the mixing and matching of modules) (Clark and Baldwin 2000). Alternatively, systems can be designed in a more integral way, especially when the benefits from specificity and performance are higher. The degree of modularity of a product is reflected in its architecture.

According to Ulrich (1995), a product architecture is "the scheme by which the functions of a product is allocated to physical components". This encompasses (i) the arranging of functions, (ii) the mapping from functions to physical components, and (iii) the specification of the corresponding interfaces. The decomposition of a product architecture in different modules is influenced by a firm's sourcing strategies and the firm's overall scope of knowledge of the system (Mikkola 2003).

Modular architectures are characterized by a one-to-one relationship between physical components and the functions of a system (Brusoni and Prencipe 2001). Such a one-to-one mapping allows a more granular (re-) combination of different functions, and thus puts fewer constraints on openness.

However, modularity also holds drawbacks. Depending on the context, its opposite, integrality can be more beneficial. Designing systems in a more modular or integral way holds a trade-off insofar as central coordination is favored to decentralized or spontaneous coordination (Langlois and Garzarelli 2008). In practice, most systems are not completely modular or integral. Similar to openness, modularity is also not a binary state but can be realized to varying degrees. As almost all systems consist of several components with some degree of coupling between them, most systems are to a certain degree, modular (Schilling 2000). Therefore, modularity is a continual concept ranging from more integral structures to more modular ones. (Campagnolo and Camuffo 2009). Designers therefore have to choose a certain degree of modularity (Mikkola 2006). Furthermore, a system can exhibit different degrees of modularity at different layers of the system architecture. Thus, different degrees of modularity could be found on the subsystem, sub-subsystems, component and sub-component level (Brusoni and Prencipe 2001).

4.5.2 Determinants of modularity

In the last section, the advantages and drawbacks of modularity have been described. In this section, the determinants of modularity in a product or system will be described.

In a literature review on the concept of modularity in management studies, Campagnolo & Camuffo (2009) identified three main streams of literature regarding the different aims of modularity: product design modularity, production system modularity and organizational design modularity. These different facets of modularity emphasize different priorities, which should be achieved by modularity: Product design modularity offers a rather technical perspective on modularity. Modularity from a production systems perspective is mainly informed by division of labor aspects both within but also among different organizations. Organizational design modularity is the most non-technical approach to modularity, as its focus is on the modularity of organizations itself. However, organizational design modularity and product modularity are not independent from each other, but they often reflect each other to some degree. For instance, there has been the proposition in the literature, that the modularity of organization reflects the modularity of the product itself (also referred to as the mirroring hypothesis) (Colfer and Baldwin 2010; MacCormack, Baldwin, and Rusnak 2012).

Another similar differentiation has been made by Baldwin & Clark (2004) who distinguish between modularity-in-use, modularity-in-design and modularity-in-production. All of these different types of modularity are beneficial at different stages of the lifecycle of a product and also aim at different actors. Modularity-in-use allows consumers to choose and combine different components and thus come up with a final product customized to their needs. An example of this kind of modularity would be different kinds of bed frames, pillows, mattresses etc. which can be manufactured by different firms but which can be combined according to the tastes of consumers. This form of modularity requires standardization of the different components so they would fit together. In contrast, modularity-in-design mainly aims to reduce design and development costs. The resulting modularization thus is dependent on organizational decisions, which reduce costs and promote efficiency. The third type of modularity, modularity-in-production aims to facilitate the production process of a system or product. One emphasis is to promote reusing different parts of a product across product lines. It also targets the users of a system, enabling the reconfiguration and customization of a product (Fixson 2001).

The different types of modularity (modularity-in-use, modularity-in-production and modularity-in-design) are not necessarily mutually exclusive, but often overlap. For instance, Ulrich (1995) distinguishes between three different types of modular architectures according to their physical interfaces: slot, bus and sectional modular architectures. Figure 5 illustrates these different types of modular architectures by means of depicting different ways how to modularize a table. These different types of modular architectures could result from both a design, as well as from a production and from a use perspective. For instance, the sectional architecture of the table in Figure 5 could be beneficial from a production, but also from a design and use perspective.

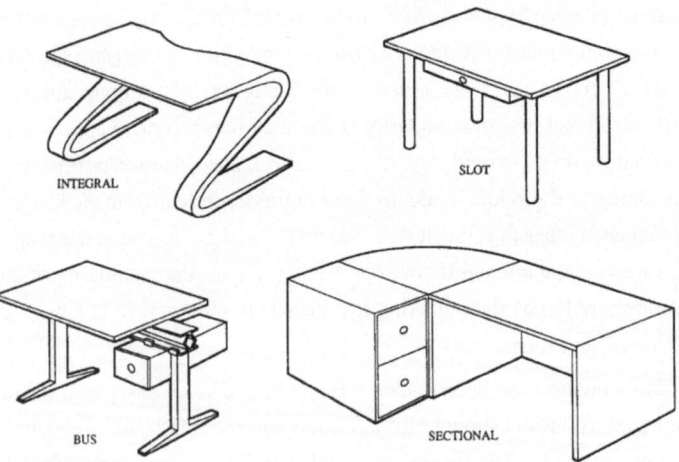

Figure 5   Types of modular architectures according to Ulrich (1995)

This chapter offered an overview of different determinants of modularity, showing that modularity of a system can be pursued by a wide range of considerations. These different considerations can also coincide with each other. For the scope of this thesis, namely open innovation in embedded systems, modularity-in-use holds particular relevance.

4.5.3   The process of modularization

Modular designs are usually not emerging ad-hoc, rather, good modular design is based on proven principles guiding the modularization process. Therefore, this chapter aims to shed light, how designers modularize a system.

It is in particular based on the work by Baldwin & Clark (2000) who describe how systems are modularized by the creation and application of a complete set of design rules. According to Baldwin & Clark (2000), to create a modular design, architects partition the design parameters into two sets: visible information and hidden information. Whereas visible information refers to design parameters whose impact takes place outside particular modules, hidden information refers to design parameters which are handled inside a module. The idea of hiding design parameters has been put forward by Parnas (1972) as a software engineering practice, naming it information hiding. It is one of the key principles of object-oriented software development (Langlois 2002), but also constitutes a general principle applicable for all kinds of systems. It aims to hide the complexity of a particular module in order to reduce the interdependencies to other modules. Thus, changing particular modules does not affect other modules. To implement the principle of information hiding, designers need to determine the boundaries of each module, and partition the system accordingly. In the following, the principle of determining the boundaries of a system's modules and hiding the complexity of each module will be referred to as *partitioning*.

Another principle strongly related to partitioning is the principle of *abstraction*. When the complexity of a certain part of the system exceeds a certain level, by defining an abstraction it would be isolated from the rest of the system and made accessible through an interface (Clark and Baldwin 2000). Whereas an abstraction can be realized via setting up interfaces, the aim of an interface is not only to hide complexity, but also to allow interaction with other parts of the system. However, an interface also hides complexity from other modules.

The third principle also mentioned in the description of abstraction is the *definition of interfaces*. Interfaces allow the coordination of interaction between different modules and resolve conflicts during the interaction of different parts of the system. An interface is similar to a treaty between different parts of a system. It is specified beforehand and known to all concerned parts of the system.

The three principles of modular design outlined above (partitioning, abstraction and interfaces) provide a frame according to which modular systems can be designed and analyzed. In particular, they inform the process of modularization and the implementation of design parameters. These principles revolve around the question, how these design parameters should be categorized in either visible or hidden information. The relationship between these two types of design information can also be arranged in a design hierarchy consisting of three levels: the global design rules, which are visible to the system as a whole. On the second level are design rules, which are only visible to a subset of a system's part. On the lowest level are the design parameters, which are only visible within modules, but otherwise are hidden. Figure 6 shows the design hierarchy with each class of design rules depicted (Clark and Baldwin 2000).

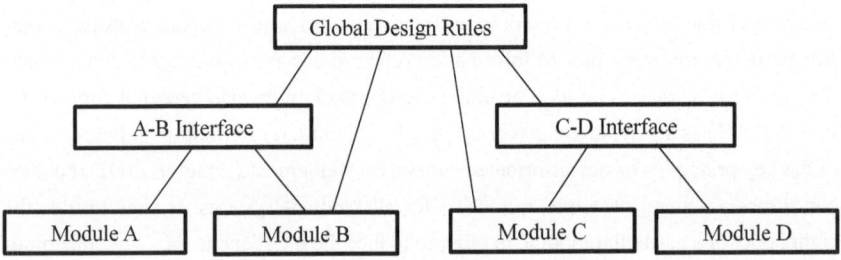

Figure 6   Design hierarchy of design rules (according to Clark & Baldwin, 2000)

The process of modularization involves determining these design rules and classifying them as visible and hidden information (Brusoni and Prencipe 2006; Clark and Baldwin 2000). They define the composition of an artifact, the way it works and how it is manufactured (Brusoni and Prencipe 2006). A complete set of design rules fully addresses the following categories of design information (Clark and Baldwin 2000):

- Architecture: determines which modules are part of the system and their functions
- Interfaces: define how modules interoperate and communicate
- Integration protocols and testing standards: procedures allowing designers the assembly of the system and determining its performance

A set of these design rules define a particular modularization (Langlois 2002). Design rules can be specified in such a way, that the result would be a closed system with proprietary interfaces but also to come up with an open system design enabling compatibility with industry standard components (Sanchez and Collins 2001). By relying on design rules which comply to open systems design, there is more potential for new entrants supplying modules and services, therefore increasing vertical disintegration (Funk 2008; Sanchez and Mahoney 1996). Thus, these rules also coordinate the activities of network participants' (Clark and Baldwin 2000). Examples for these rules are standards, protocols defining information exchange, policies or contracts (Eisenmann et al. 2008).

The design rules perspective thus defines certain rules, which should be applied to achieve a certain design goal. This perspective further elaborates the frame according to which modular systems the design of systems for open innovation can be analyzed.

The relationship between modularity and distributed innovation has for instance been explored by Henkel, Baldwin, & Shih (2012), who introduce the concept of intellectual property (IP) modularity which balances distributed innovation processes and the firms need to capture value. When designing a modular system, a firm must simultaneously consider the technical boundaries of the modules and the corresponding IP in each module. In a system architecture which is "IP modular", "the technical boundaries of modules are co-extensive with IP status" (Henkel, Baldwin, and Shih 2012). Therefore, the consideration of IP issues leads to certain design rules influenced by IP considerations. Similarly to IP, other factors also constitute design rules which influence the modularity of a system. Henkel et al. (2012) also mention safety as one such aspect, however, they do not further state how this aspect would be considered.

Identifying and analyzing the impact of such factors is crucial for understanding how to open ES for OI. Therefore, the research design in Chapter III of this thesis will also be informed by this aspect.

Based on the design principles (partitioning, abstraction and interfaces) and the design rules perspective laid out in this chapter, the next chapter discusses, the implications of openness on modularity.

4.5.4 Modularity and openness

After introducing the concept of modularity and presenting the process of modularization, this chapter builds on these foundations and shows the influence of openness on the design of modular systems. This will be accomplished by building on the three main design principles for modular systems outlined in 5.5.3 (partitioning, interfaces and abstraction). Each of these principles will be further elaborated and it will be discussed how these principles can be used to facilitate openness.

4.5.4.1 Partitioning

Partitioning is the process of distributing a system's functions on particular modules. Designers choose a particular approach to partitioning according to different goals. The different forms of modularity presented in section 4.5.2 (modularity-in-design, modularity-in-production and modularity-in-use) are examples for goals, which dictate the approach to partition a system. The approach, which comes closest to realize openness would be modularity-in-use. By following modularity-in-use, the system would be partitioned in such a way, that it would allow the later addition of modules by the user. In order to enable users to change certain modules, a different approach may be chosen. For instance, the notion of IP modularity as described 4.5.3 would lead to a partitioning according to different levels of IP protection. This partitioning strategy would allow realizing partial openness.

Further input for partitioning systems according to openness considerations arises from the platform literature, which has been discussed in section 4.4. According to Tushman & Murmann (1998), platforms are usually partitioned into core components and peripheral components. The core components are characterized by tight coupling to other subsystems with low variety, which remain stable over a long period of time. In contrast, the peripheral components are more subject to changes and substitution, as they exhibit higher variety and looser connections to other parts of the system. Design decisions on core parts thus have a greater impact on other parts of the systems, whereas changes regarding peripheral parts have less impact (MacCormack, Baldwin, and Rusnak 2010).

Dividing a system into core parts, which are stable and peripheral parts, which are subject to changes, allows to direct external innovation to certain parts of the system (the peripheral parts). However, firms also have to consider other factors when partitioning for openness.

When firms partition their systems according to openness characteristics, a key factor they need to consider is the protection of intellectual property. According to Henkel et al. (2012), systems should not be partitioned only according to technical or organizational criteria, but should also consider IP and value capture aspects. By using a case study approach, they found that firms can at the same time gain from distributed value creation through openness, and ensuring value capture, by partitioning their systems in accordance with their IP regime. Next to IP aspects, Henkel et al. (2012) also raise other issues which would need to be considered when partitioning a system, such as safety aspects.

4.5.4.2 Interfaces

Modularizing a system involves facilitating communication between different components along standardized interfaces (Clark and Baldwin 2000; Langlois 2002). According to Baldwin & Clark (2000) ,"an interface is a pre-established way to resolve potential conflicts between interacting parts of a design" The types of interactions which take place between different modules can be categorized into four types (Pimmler and Eppinger 1994):

- **Spatial**: refers to adjacency or orientation between two elements.
- **Energy**: refers to energy transfer between two elements.
- **Information**: refers to information or signal exchange between two elements.
- **Material**: refers to materials exchange between two elements.

In the following discussion about interfaces, the term interface will be used, but especially with the focus on spatial interfaces and interfaces for transferring information. With embedded systems consisting both of software and hardware parts, these are the two main types of interfaces relevant for this thesis.

When developing a module, the module designer needs to decide to which degree users need to be able to interact with that specific module. This results in an interface specification. Another important characteristic of interfaces concerning openness is whether they are standardized. More specifically, an interface is standardized when the protocol standards are used widely throughout an industry in contrast to non-standardized interfaces which would be firm-specific (Cabigiosu, Zirpoli, and Camuffo 2012; Fine, Golany, and Naseraldin 2005). Standardizing interfaces also constitute a way of sharing design information for external innovators and at the same time create rules to govern the enhancement of a system (Chen and Liu 2005; Simcoe 2006). Therefore, standardization of interfaces is essential for mix-and-matching of modules and enables externals to integrate additional modules (Clark and Baldwin 2000), whereas modules internally may remain non-standardized (Cabigiosu, Zirpoli, and Camuffo 2012). In terms of openness, it can be distinguished between the options of standard creations and the adoption of existing standards (Dedrick and West 2003).

From a management perspective, the creation of standards is a way to spark network effects and to spur technology adoption. Different firms often compete with different standards, leading to a single dominant technology of the creation of an industry standard. An alternative to competing standards is a joint development of standards by standard-setting organizations consisting of different firms working together on developing a specific standard (Simcoe 2006).

To invite participation and innovation for a particular modular system, firms can also adopt existing open standards (Simcoe 2006). Adopting standards allows benefitting from externals investing in a particular technology as well as access to complementary assets (Dedrick and West 2003).

In the software domain, interfaces are usually offered in the form of APIs. These can be seen as generic interfaces allowing other modules to communicate with other parts of the system. An API often provides a variety of methods and attributes which can be accessed to implement a certain behavior of a component. The designer of an API can decide which internal methods of a system or a module will be accessible through the API. Therefore, by exposing certain functions and properties of a system through an API, designers can also determine the degree of openness of certain software modules.

4.5.4.3 Abstraction

Complex systems are usually hierarchical with different levels representing different levels of abstraction which built on lower levels (Booch 1994). For computer systems, the principle of abstraction is especially prevalent. Most computer systems are partitioned in several layers, as it has already been discussed in 4.2. The lowest level constitutes the hardware layer, which is made accessible on the operating system layer via the software/hardware interface. On top of the OS layer resides the application layer, which accesses the capabilities of the OS via APIs. Application developers therefore do not need to know details about the hardware layer or about the specifics of the operating system, but access the functions of the system through the APIs offered by the OS.

Basically all of today's PCs follow this architecture, thus enabling independent third-party development. The Windows and Linux OS platforms can both be seen as examples where this partitioning into separate layers resulted in a huge variety of different applications supplied by third parties. From a design rules perspective, abstraction layers put some of the design rules on the secondary level, making them visible for parts of the system (inside a layer) but not to the outside layers.

By specifying the interfaces between the different layers, system designers can control which parts of the system are accessible for externals. Besides facilitating systems development, this also attracts more external developers who are not experts for a certain system type and with its particular characteristics. Regarding openness of ES, this constitutes a major factor in attracting externals, as the different types of ES often possess very specific characteristics.

A study where openness has been explored along different layers of a system has been conducted by Anvaari & Jansen (2010) who evaluate the architectural openness of mobile software platforms for third-party developers. They classify architectural openness according to changes users are allowed to make to the architecture of a system based on the different layers of a mobile software platform. They differentiate between the kernel, middleware and application layer. On each of these layers, external would be allowed to conduct the following operations:

- Integrate a layer: Making use of a layer
- Extend a layer: Add additional functionality to a particular layer
- Modify a layer: Changing certain parts of a layer

Another example of the use of abstraction in computer systems is programming languages. Whereas earlier programming languages were still pretty close to the underlying hardware, over time, more and more higher-level programming languages have evolved. These languages facilitate development as they abstract technical details of the underlying system and allow for consistent software development across different platforms.

Both these two examples of abstraction in computer systems greatly facilitate openness for third-party innovation, as externals therefore need less expertise concerning the inner workings of a system.

5   Summary of part II

This part presented the theoretical foundations guiding this thesis. In the first step, the primary themes of this thesis, namely embedded systems as well as open innovation have been laid out. By combining these two perspectives, two different forms of open innovation in ES have been identified:

- Open innovation in embedded systems by opening embedded systems

- Open innovation in embedded systems without opening embedded systems

Whereas the second approach does not require the ES firm to actively pursue OI, the first approach raises a variety of challenges for the ES firm. It came out, that pursuing OI by opening ES faces particular challenges, which are not present in other domains. First of all, ES are often not designed in such a way that it allows externals to contribute complementary innovations. The presentation of ES has also revealed specific technical characteristics of ES, which challenge the application of open innovation practices. These characteristics are for instance dependability (safety, security, reliability etc.) as well as real-time requirements. In addition, organizational aspects such as the protection of IP or liability issues constitute further challenges when opening ES.

To tackle the organizational and technical challenges for OI in ES, it was drawn on extant literature to elaborate the notion of openness. After introducing and elaborating openness, literature on openness in computer systems has been reviewed. Based on these foundations, the implications of the characteristics of ES on openness have been discussed. Whereas this discussion offers a clear picture of the challenges, which need to be considered, it does not offer solutions to solve these challenges.

To provide a frame for the analysis of these challenges, two main literature streams have been presented: theory on platforms as well as on modularity. The platform literature exemplifies the challenges when opening an external system for open innovation. As ES, which are opened, are basically platforms, this literature helps to increase the understanding of openness settings such as ES. Especially, it allowed to refine this thesis' view on openness and its underlying economics.

Borrowing from the literature on platforms, open innovation for ES takes place around a core part with external innovators coming up with complementary innovation around the ES core. A key question for firms aiming to allow open innovation is to define, which parts of their systems constitute the core, which would remain unchanged. By varying the degree of openness, firms can thus control, what constitutes the core of their system and what parts are opened for external innovators. However, specific approaches, which take into account ES characteristics, cannot be inferred from the platform literature.

To be able to come up with approaches towards opening ES for OI, a second theoretical perspective was needed. For this purpose, modularity theory has been chosen as it explains how systems are designed in accordance with openness considerations. The consideration of modularity especially focused on the principles of modular design (architecture and partitioning, interfaces and abstraction) which will later be used in the empirical part.

For a comprehensive exploration of OI in ES, the second approach towards OI in ES (OI without opening ES) also needs to be addressed. Whereas the first approach enables OI at specific parts of their systems, this approach aims to deal with OI which does not take place along the explicit extensions points provided by the ES firm. Considering this form of OI holds potential for ES firms to further refine their OI strategy.

Part III

Empirical Studies

1 Research design

In the following section, the research design of this thesis is laid out. To provide the context for the research questions addressed in this thesis, a short summary of the findings in the literature will be provided. This allows to more clearly show the research gap. Then, the research methods that will be used addressing the research questions will be described.

As it has been outlined in Part II Chapter 3., open innovation denotes the phenomenon of firms opening their innovation processes to allow outsiders to participate in the creation of innovations. In technical settings such an opening of innovation processes would not be enough, as externals would not only contribute ideas but also change the underlying system themselves. Therefore, enabling open innovation for technical systems, such as embedded systems, also requires opening of the underlying technical system. Thus, the overall research question of this thesis is as follows: *"How can Open Innovation be enabled for ES?"* (Main RQ).

The overall research question can be divided in several individual research questions and is answered by several studies.

The first part of this thesis' results will focus on open innovation for ES, which have been explicitly opened for OI. To explore this form of open innovation, a clear understanding of openness in ES is required. In Part II Chapter 4 the notion of openness has already been elaborated based on the literature. To put openness in the context of this thesis and to explain its significance for open innovation in embedded systems, it was drawn on existing literature on platforms. This literature constitutes one of the main sources dealing with technical systems, which are opened for third parties. Embedded systems, which are opened, can be seen as specific examples of platforms. Furthermore, platforms already incorporate the notion of partial openness, which aims to open ES to a certain degree, while at the same time leave other parts closed. Existing literature thus focuses on mechanisms to implement partial openness, to structure the system in a closed core and open parts. This allows to control to which parts externals are able to contribute. In this regard, this literature stream provided valuable insights towards understanding the phenomenon of open innovation in ES.

This thesis therefore builds on existing literature on platforms and enhances it by analyzing the case of embedded systems. The literature on platforms offers diverse studies e.g. on mobile phone platforms, but does not address the specific domain of ES. Part II,

Chapter II.4.3 has shown, that ES exhibit specific technical characteristics, which crucially influence system design and also influence potential open innovation. Therefore, an understanding of the implications of these characteristic on OI is required. This leads to the research question *How do the technical characteristics of ES constrain or enable open innovation practices" (RQ 1)*.

Answering this research question provides the basis for exploring how ES firms actually open themselves for OI. This opening process has two different facets: First of all, firms need to open their open innovation processes in accordance with the technical requirements of ES but also in accordance to organizational requirements. From an organizational point of view, one of the primary issue firms are facing is how to benefit from OI without giving away too much knowledge to outsiders. Furthermore, they need to decide which parts of the system they want to supply themselves and to what degree they would allow externals to contribute. Besides these decisions, other organizational issues influencing openness would be liability issues or the need for external expertise. Thus, the opening of OI processes requires determining to which external actors and to which degree the OI processes can be opened. Firms thus have to decide to whom and to which they degree they want to open their ES. This raises the question: *"How can firms pursue the opening of their systems and their organizations to enable open innovation?"* (RQ 2). This research question has been tackled in Chapter 4.

Whereas the focus of this study lies on the organizational opening for open innovation, it does not take the technical opening of ES into account. Therefore, the next study needs to address the technical opening of ES for OI. As a theoretical framework, this is guided by theory on modularity, which has been laid out in II.4.5. In this chapter, it was described according to which principles systems are modularized. Using this theoretical background, the design impact of openness on the modularity of an ES can be described. In particular, it needs to be addressed how the specific requirements of ES influence the technical opening of ES. The research question addressing this research gap is as follows:

How can embedded systems be technically opened to enable open innovation? (RQ3)

These three research questions are all dealing with open innovation enabled by the ES firm – as it requires the active opening of ES by the ES firm.

Although specifically opening an ES for open innovation would greatly facilitate OI, open innovation can also take place without specifically opening ES. Externals may also innovate in unanticipated ways not covered by the current openness strategy. This may occur rather sporadically or under certain circumstances, but also needs to be explored for a comprehensive understanding of OI in ES. One reason for exploring OI in ES without openness is that it allows a better understanding of the circumstances, which are required for OI. Besides, this would also allow them to adjust their opening strategy. Therefore, the fourth study of the empirical part covers cases where the ES was not explicitly opened. The underlying research question for this study is "*What forms of open innovation can be found in ES without opening ES?*" (RQ4). The research objective in this study is to provide a classification of open innovation in embedded systems without opening ES (Chapter 5).

Table 4 summarizes the presented research questions and gives an overview of the subsequent studies answering the particular research question. In addition, Figure 7 depicts the research design with reference to the underlying literature perspectives.

Table 4   Overview of research questions and studies

Research question	Chapter / Study	Method
How do the technical characteristics of ES constrain or enable open innovation practices?	Chapter 2	Conceptual Study
How can firms pursue the opening of their systems and their organizations to enable open innovation?	Chapter 3	Explorative Interview Study
How can embedded systems be technically opened to enable open innovation?	Chapter 4	Case Studies
What forms of open innovation can be found in ES without opening ES?	Chapter 5	Case Vignettes

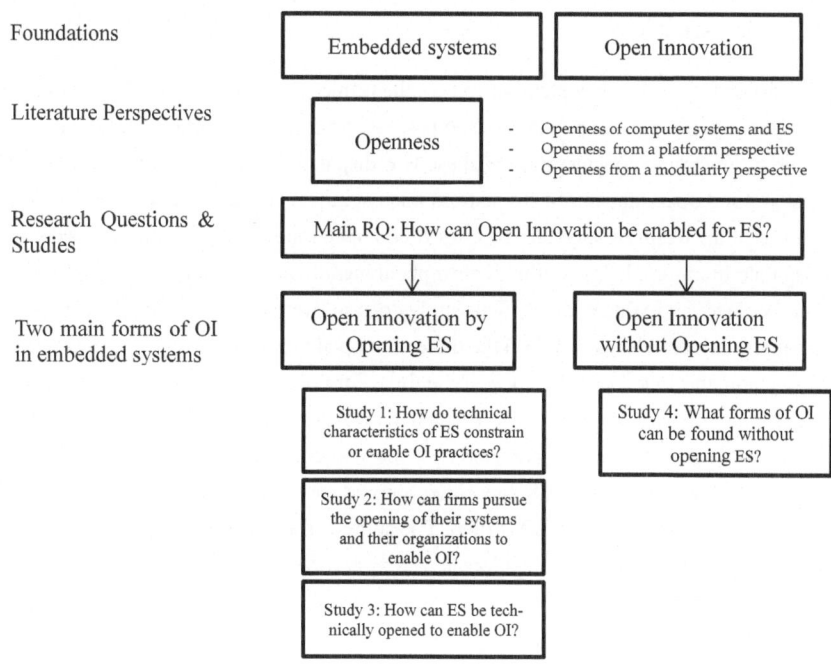

Figure 7   Overview of research design

2   Study 1 - Exploring open innovation processes in the ES domain[2]

In the theoretical part of this thesis, the paradigm of open innovation as well as the three core open innovation processes according to Gassmann & Enkel (2004) have been presented. The following conceptual study builds on these three core OI processes and aims to explore the potential of the three core open innovation processes in the context of ES. The underlying research question of this study is as follows: *"How do these technical characteristics constrain or enable open innovation practices?"*

The study is structured in the following parts: First of all, the research design will be presented in 2.1, whereon follows the conceptual analysis based on literature (2.2). The findings elicited from this analysis will then be presented in the results section (2.3). The last part of the study is formed by the conclusion, which will discuss the results (2.4).

---

[2] An earlier version of this chapter was presented at the *GeNeMe Conference*, Dresden, Germany (2012) and published as Soeldner, Danzinger, Roth, & Moeslein (2012).

2.1   Research design

The following study conceptually explores the influences of the technical characteristics of ES on the three core open innovation processes. So far, the current literature does not offer an integrated consideration of these two disparate literature streams of embedded systems and open innovation. To address this gap, the study at hand analyzes the implications of the technical characteristics of ES on open innovation. Contrasting two sets of disparate literature, helps to illuminate a phenomenon and derive implications for practice (Webster and Watson 2002). This study does so by analyzing the implications of the technical characteristics of ES on the three core open innovation processes presented by Gassmann and Enkel (2004). Each of the three core open innovation processes has certain characteristics, which will be presented in the next section. The following discussion shows to what degree these characteristics apply to companies, which produce ES. The technical characteristics of ES can either support or constrain the applicability of the three core OI processes in the ES field. The sources for the conceptual study are based both on literature on open innovation as well as on ES literature.

2.2   The three core open innovation processes

As it has been written in II.3, Gassmann and Enkel (2004) categorized open innovation into three core processes: the outside-in process, the inside-out process and the coupled process. The outside-in process aims to integrate external actors like suppliers or customers to benefit from external knowledge by increasing the innovativeness. By choosing the inside-out process, companies externalize some of their knowledge in order to commercialize their ideas faster on the market than it would be possible internally. This can for instance be done by licensing intellectual property (IP) and/or providing knowledge to other companies in order to benefit from multiplying technology (Gassmann and Enkel 2004). The coupled process combines both of these processes (incorporating external knowledge and bringing ideas to the market) by working together with other firms in strategic networks. In these strategic networks, knowledge is created through relationships between specific partners, e.g. in consortia, joint ventures or alliances (Gassmann and Enkel 2004). The characteristics of firms relying on the three core OI processes according to Gassmann & Enkel (2004) can be seen in Table 5. These characteristics have been collected from a sample of 124 companies. Therefore, they provide a generalized view on the applicability of the three processes.

Table 5   Characteristics of the core OI processes according to Gassmann & Enkel (2004)

Outside-In process	Inside-Out process	Coupled process
Low tech industry for similar technology acquisition	(basic) research-driven company	Standard setting (pre dominant design)
act as knowledge brokers and/or knowledge creators	Objectives like decreasing the fixed costs of R&D, branding, setting standards via spillovers	Increasing returns (e.g. in the mobile industry through multiplying technology)
highly modular products		Alliance with complementary partners
high knowledge intensity		Complementary products with critical interfaces
		Relational view of the firm

Based on the characteristics of these three core innovation processes, it will be analyzed how they can be implemented in the context of embedded systems. For this purpose, the implications of the characteristics of ES on characteristics of firms relying on the three core OI processes will be shown. The characteristics of ES have been presented in II.2. In summary, ES are characterized by dependability and real-time characteristics; they make use of sensors and actuators; are reactive systems, consist of analog and digital parts (hybrid systems); are subject to efficiency requirements; often have a dedicated user interface and are dedicated toward a specific application. The next section explores the influences of these properties of ES on each characteristic of the three core OI processes as depicted in Table 5.

2.2.1   Implications of the characteristics of ES on the outside-in process

Low-tech industry for similar technology acquisition

According to Gassmann & Enkel (2004), firms applying outside-in processes, mostly stem from low tech industries where externals provide input for developing new technologies. These companies would be able to benefit from spillovers from higher tech industries. However, in the meantime, the paradigm of OI has also spread to more high-tech intensive fields (the smart phone which is based on external apps constitutes such an example). Especially in markets with high competition, firms need to differentiate themselves with innovative functionalities. Firms producing embedded systems could be found both in low tech as in high tech areas. Those ES could be quite primitive regarding their functionality, therefore only low cost hardware would be needed and the software only would have to fulfill simple tasks. However, they could also be quite complex as for example in the automotive domain. Therefore, there do not seem to be direct relations between the characteristics of ES and this characteristic of the outside-in process. However, further validation needs to be carried out to provide a comprehensive answer.

Knowledge brokers and/or knowledge creators

In the past, firms deciding on the outside-in process were SMEs which had the role of knowledge creators or brokers to bigger companies (Gassmann and Enkel 2004), however, Gassmann & Enkel (2004) state that this refers to past data and company size does not play a significant role anymore for firms being knowledge brokers and/or creators. Thus, this characteristic will not be explored further in this study.

Modularity

According to Baldwin & Henkel (2011), "modular systems are made up of components that are highly interdependent within sub-blocks, called modules, and largely independent across those sub-blocks" (Baldwin and Henkel 2011). Complex systems can be subdivided into discrete parts communicating with each other by relying on standardized interfaces as part of a standardized architecture (Langlois 2002). Due to the independence among different modules, changes in a specific module normally do not influence other modules (Baldwin and Henkel 2011). Concerning product design, modularity is beneficial when flexibility and rapid innovation are demanded (Sendil K Ethiraj and Levinthal 2004; Ulrich and Eppinger 2000). The increase in product innovation is attributed mainly to autonomous and modular innovation (Clark and Baldwin 2000; Sendil K Ethiraj and Levinthal 2004). ES typically consist of several separate layers (Noergaard 2005), thus enabling modularity. Although a layered design provides abstractions from lower levels, applications built on top of the ES architecture must not be allowed to violate real-time constraints and dependability requirements. Modularity is also limited in ES due to its hybrid nature. Due to its strong need for attunement, for instance because of RT requirements, software and hardware in ES often needs to be designed simultaneously (Fernandes et al. 2009). Often, the modularization is centered on intellectual property (IP). IP-oriented modularization can be used as a tactic to balance value creation and value capture when opening their systems (Henkel and Baldwin 2010). Therefore, decisions regarding the externalization of IP are mainly dependent on business model decision. According to Henkel & Baldwin (2010), providing open access to some parts of the platform can be the most effective way to increase innovation and value creation in some instances. Decisions on giving up control over intellectual property in ES however, is not only a matter of value creation and value capture, but is also determined by characteristics of ES as well. As cost efficiency is one of the characteristics of ES, externalizing IP for complementary development could also help ES firms to reduce development costs. Another motivation for licensing is the potential reuse of components. However, for safety-critical systems, higher risks are involved, as failures often can be found at interfaces of logically correct components (Saglietti 2004).

Knowledge intensity

Firms with high knowledge intensity often tend to outside-in innovation, when the required know-how cannot be acquired inside the firm (Gassmann and Enkel 2004). Above, it was mentioned that lower tech industries not possessing certain expertise may also gain from knowledge derived from higher tech industries. Developing for ES requires possessing extensive domain knowledge, therefore, ES developers are usually control engineers and mechanical engineers, which have a thorough understanding of the physical characteristics of the device and the environment where it operates (Liggesmeyer and Trapp 2009). As ES are hybrid systems, the initial design of ES involves both hardware and software design. The tight coupling of HW and SW in ES requires more know-how than traditional software development (Henzinger and Sifakis 2007), increasing with the complexity of the ES. For systems requiring a high degree of domain knowledge, open innovation processes thus are confined to experts, especially when it comes to the core functionalities of the system. For the development of additional applications on top of the base system, the complexity involved can be reduced by providing interfaces for external developers. This has for instance taken place in the smartphone domain, where the base system is essentially closed, but interfaces for application development are provided. For devices in which the ES part played only a minor role so far, not so much expertise would be required. However, when they plan to implement more innovative functionalities through software, additional expertise would be needed. Sensors and actuators are a domain for which it could be beneficial to acquire external expertise, because writing software for them requires developers to have knowledge about the physical characteristics of the device and its environment which may not be present in the company. It can be seen that implementing the outside-in process is in some aspects restricted by ES characteristics.

2.2.2 Implications of the characteristics of ES on the inside-out process

Research-driven companies with objectives like decreasing the fixed costs of R&D, branding, setting standards via spillovers

According to Gassmann & Enkel (2004), companies relying on the inside-out process are mostly research-driven companies with broad application fields, which aim at reducing the fixed costs of R&D and mitigating risks by sharing them with partners. However, due to the dedication to a specific function in many ES, embedded systems are often seen in terms of their cost efficiency and not as a source of innovation. Therefore, most ES do not have broad application fields. However, with the tendency of ES to become cheaper and at the same time having more and more performance, the demand for innovative functions is increasing (Broy 2006). Furthermore, ES firms are not necessarily research-driven companies, as for example consumer goods manufacturers often compete more on prices than on new technologies. However, in domains such as the automotive domain, more and more innovative functions are implemented via software (Ebert and Jones 2009). Furthermore, the increasing performance of microchips combined with decreasing costs lead to a higher demand of innovative functions by the customers. Additionally, in highly competitive markets, focusing more on innovative functions could help firms to differentiate themselves. For branding, when firms have internal capabilities for the development and commercialization of products but do not possess a brand on a specific market, no implications of the ES characteristics were found. The goal of setting standards will be analyzed separately in the next section as it is also a characteristic determining the coupled process.

Standard setting

Standards for embedded systems can be divided into market-specific standards, general-purpose standards and standards which apply to both of these categories. Market-specific standards refer to standards encountered in specific markets (Noergaard 2005). Such standards can for instance be defined by industry consortiums such as AUTOSAR in the automotive industry. One of the goals of AUTOSAR is to enable the interoperability among different components (software, hardware and tools) (Sangiovanni-Vincentelli and Di Natale 2007). General-purpose standards are not limited to a specific class of embedded devices, but could be adopted in other ES and non-ES, for instance standards referring to programming languages (Noergaard 2005). For ES firms, relying on standards facilitates involving external actors for open innovation processes. For instance, the

Java language is such a standard which works with a high variety of different hardware architectures (Noergaard 2005). Therefore, efficiency as a property of ES could be increased by the implementation of standards in the design of ES. In terms of opening embedded systems, the question of standards is crucial in order to ensure interoperability. It is of particular relevance in complex ES like in the automotive domain where many suppliers and partners work together in order to provide an integrated solution. Therefore, for open innovation in the business-to-business sector, the implementation of market-specific standards in addition to general purpose-standards needs to be ensured. However, due to the tight coupling of embedded software to the hardware, standardization is often only possible to a certain degree (Ziegler and Müller 2008).

Based on this analysis, the need of standards provides only minor challenges to the Inside-Out process. However, the setting of standards of ES firms can be seen as a requirement for external participation.

2.2.3 Implications of the characteristics of ES on the coupled process

Standard Setting

The characteristic of standard setting has already been analyzed for the Inside-Out process and applies to the coupled process as well.

Increasing returns by multiplying technology

Increasing returns can be exploited by firms through multiplying their technology by setting industry standards, as it has for instance been taken place in the mobile industry with the MMS or the UMTS standard or the polyphone ring tunes (Gassmann and Enkel 2004). In order to establish those standards, industry-wide strategic alliances are required. This strategy is of particular relevance in the case of network effects where the value for customer increases when more participants join the network (Parker and Van Alstyne 2005). With the increasing connectivity of ES, telecommunication producers could play a key role (Ziegler and Müller 2008) in providing solutions. Implications of the characteristics of ES on how firms can profit by multiplying technology were not found in this study.

Alliances with complementary partners

Alliances with complementary partners might be in some cases a more promising approach for ES producers than a broader opening their system to external partners. Especially, when the integration of components developed by other parties is subject to high complexity, having strong ties to these partners would be beneficial to manage the integration process. For instance, in the case of automotive software, the integration of components of safety-critical components is a major challenge (Sangiovanni-Vincentelli and Di Natale 2007). Due to the hybrid nature of ES, software engineering and mechanical and electrical engineering are part of overall system engineering, which makes coordination more challenging (Graaf, Lormans, and Toetenel 2003). Therefore, with increasing complexity of the system, alliances would be preferable to forms of loose cooperation. Regarding the different layers of the embedded system architecture, the more critical parts of the systems are affected (in terms of dependability and real-time requirements), the more ES firms should seek closer alliances. According to a study of the significance of the ES sector in Germany conducted by the Bitkom industry association (Ziegler and Müller 2008), many ES firms see potentials for synergy among firms from different industries which face similar challenges.

Complementarity of products

Drawing from the research on platforms, complementarity is an important design goal in two-sided markets, with the platform owners differing from the application developers (Haruvy, Sethi, and Zhou 2008). One of the motivations for opening technologies is to stimulate the development of complementary products. For instance, revealing source code is a means to increase complementarity (Henkel 2006). However, simple ES architectures often do not provide software layers abstracting from the hardware layers to enable application development (Noergaard 2005). By providing additional software layers, for instance an operating system layer, developing applications is facilitated. By providing interfaces for developers (APIs), it is easier for application developers to develop complementary applications. However, those interfaces are often not offered by the manufacturers of embedded devices due to economic reasons and technical challenges. For platform vendors, it is often more profitable to provide their own applications. Furthermore, they often do not want to lose control over their platform (Gunter and Alur 2003). The opening of ES in the form of providing interfaces bears risks as well, especially security risks, e.g. viruses and worms (Heiser 2008). Besides these security threats, safety issues also prevent firms from allowing complementary SW development. For example, in the automotive industry, when software stems from different suppliers, the integration of safety-critical sub-components requires strong methodology and discipline to control the compliance to this methodology of partners and suppliers (Sangiovanni-Vincentelli and Di Natale 2007).

Relational view of the firm

The characteristic "Relational View of the firm" denotes a cultural aspect of firms, namely the ability to sustain "the right balance of give and take" which is required when working in strategic alliances and joint ventures (Gassmann and Enkel 2004). Direct influences of the characteristics of ES on this aspect have not been found in this analysis.

Similar to the Outside-In process, the characteristics of ES are crucial to the successful implementation of the Inside-Out process. Of particular importance in this context is to ensure tight coordination between the firms and external partners.

2.3 Results

The results of this analysis are depicted in Table 6. It shows how the different characteristics of ES affect the three core OI processes. Whereas this analysis brought forward various implications on the characteristics of the three core OI processes, not every characteristic of the three core OI processes is affected by the specific settings in ES. Furthermore, the results based on this analysis still need to be empirically validated.

Table 6   Implications of the characteristics of ES on the three core OI processes

	Outside-In Process	Inside-Out Process	Coupled Process
Dependability	Dependability more difficult to ensure with high modularity; Safety requirements limit licensing possibilities		Tight coordination among partners or in alliances required because of dependability; Safety requirements limit potential complementarity
Efficiency	Aim of cost efficiency could better be attained by outside licensing	Required efficiency drives implementation and development of standards	Required efficiency drives implementation and development of standards
Sensors and actuators	External know-how could be beneficial for sensors and actuators due to high knowledge intensity		

Real-time con-straints	Design for modularity needs to ensure real-time constraints, e.g. by tight coordination with partners		
Reactive systems			
Hybrid systems	Higher knowledge intensity due to dichotomy of HW and SW, which could be met by external know how; Physical constraints hinder separate, modular design	Tight coupling of HW and SW complicates standard implementation	Tight coupling of HW and SW complicates standard implementation; Hybrid aspects add to complexity and therefore needs strong coordination
Dedicated user interface			
Dedicated towards a specific application			Long-term trend in ES design could be towards multiple applications and complementarity

The results show, that especially the outside-in and the coupled process are affected by the characteristics of embedded systems, whereas the inside-out process seems to be more independent from ES characteristics. A factor that requires more exploration is the relation between some of the firm characteristics implementing these OI processes. For instance, setting standards can be seen as a facilitator of modularity and complementarity, especially when other parties are involved. Furthermore, as it has already been mentioned, not all kinds of ES have to fulfill these characteristics to the same degree. Therefore, some aspects could be more or less relevant when considering a specific type of ES. Regarding the outside-in process, there are some characteristics of ES posing challenges for the involvement of external actors. Especially dependability requirements, real-time constraints and the hybrid composition of ES require tight cooperation between the involved parties. In cases, where these characteristics are not as critical, looser forms of coordination would be imaginable. One aspect of ES presented in all of the three OI processes is the aim to achieve higher efficiency, especially in terms of costs. However, as efficiency in ES development has traditionally been seen as equipping a device with cheap hardware with limited capabilities, there was scarcely any potential for innovative applications. By relying on open innovation on the software side, additional efficiency can be gained, even though more hardware resources would be required.

Although these results still have to be empirically validated, but this classification serves as a first understanding about the influence of ES characteristics on open innovation processes. Thus, it constitutes a frame to systematically discuss relevant issues in opening up ES.

2.4 Conclusion

As research concerning the combination of open innovation with a technical perspective outside the open source development is still scarce, this study contributes to understand the applicability of open innovation in technical settings, in this case in the field of embedded systems. Based on the characteristics of firms implementing the three core innovation processes according to Gassmann & Enkel (2004), the implications of the characteristics of embedded systems on the applicability of open innovation in this field were analyzed. As a result, it came out, how these characteristic either facilitate or hinder the three open innovation processes. Of these three innovation processes, each of them is applicable in the context of ES, with particular applicability of the outside-in process and the coupled process. Ensuring the requirements of ES poses some challenges. As this analysis was based on the characteristics of firms implementing the three core OI processes, it provides guidance for ES firms in the implementation of OI processes. Further research should focus on validating the proposed framework and exploring missing factors of ES influencing OI as well as identifying missing characteristics of ES firms, which determine the applicability of OI. As embedded systems are quite diverse, the evaluation should incorporate different classes of embedded systems to provide a comprehensive picture.

3 Study 2 - Organizational opening of ES companies for open innovation[3]

The following study explores the organizational aspects of open innovation in ES. In particular, it aims to answer the research question *"How can firms pursue the opening of their systems and their organizations to enable open innovation?"*. The study is divided into the following sections: Firstly, the research design is presented, consisting of the data collection (3.1.1) and the data analysis (3.1.2) sections. Then the results of the study

---

[3] An earlier version of this chapter was presented at the *19th Americas Conference on Information Systems*, Chicago, USA (2013) and published as Soeldner, Roth, Danzinger, & Moeslein (2013).

are presented thematically in 3.2, 3.3 and 3.4., followed by the discussion (3.5) and the conclusion in 3.6.

3.1 Research Design

Although there are a variety of factors, both technical and organizational, which are described in the literature, the concept of ES openness remains unexplored. To the authors' best knowledge, there is no comprehensive overview of technical and organizational factors influencing potential openness of ES. Thus, the goal is to explore how firms can pursue the opening of their embedded systems and their organization in order to enable open innovation.

In order to address the research question, a qualitative research approach based on explorative expert interviews was chosen. This method was selected to gain an in-depth understanding of the phenomenon by incorporating experts from different backgrounds in the field of embedded systems (Creswell 1994; King and Horrocks 2010).

3.1.1 Data collection

In total, 12 interviews with representatives from 12 different organizations focusing on the development of ES have been conducted using a semi-structured interview guideline. The interviews took place between June and September 2012. The experts were selected based on their expertise in the field of ES from both a technical as well as a business perspective. Ten of the experts work for international companies, one participant works for a national company based in Germany and one expert holds a position as a full-time researcher in the field of ES. Table 7 provides an overview about the organizations' focus and the position of the participants. The length of the interviews was between 45 and 110 minutes. Subsequently, the recorded interviews were transcribed verbatim. The interviews were started with a general question about current trends and challenges in the field of ES. To prepare a common ground, the first part of the interviews referred to the concept of ES openness. The interviewees were asked about approaches to ES openness and about different degrees of ES openness. In the second part, technical aspects relating to ES openness were explored. In the third part, the organizational aspects relating to ES were discussed.

Table 7 Interviewees and their organizations

Role of interviewee	Focus of the organization
Manager, business development	Product engineering in healthcare / telecommunication
Project manager, SW development	Electrical engineering / Automotive
BU manager	Consulting in software & product engineering
Department manager	ES producer in the automotive industry
CEO	Software development in the fields of automotive and medical engineering
Senior software engineer	ES software development
CTO	Consulting in software & product engineering
CEO	GUI development for embedded devices
Researcher	Computer science chair at University, Embedded systems
Consultant, R&D	Electrical engineering for industrial machines
Senior consultant	ES software development
CEO	Consulting for smart products

3.1.2 Data analysis

All interview transcripts were analyzed in-depth by two independent researchers during September until November 2012. Data coding and qualitative content analysis was supported by the qualitative research software MAXQDA based on content analysis procedures to code data (Mayring 2002). Coding was done by two independent parties and then compared by following an analyst triangulation process (Yin 2008). If data collected from the various sources were inconsistent or contradictory, the author went back to the interviewee to clarify issues and compared the findings with existing literature. The content analysis was driven by the research question. In literature, openness has been considered in the context of platforms, mainly considering business model aspects. Here, openness in the context of ES was analyzed considering technical and organizational factors influencing ES openness. For data analysis, the study relied on the summarizing content analysis according to Mayring (2002). For the summarizing content analysis, three steps were conducted. First of all, the coded text sections were paraphrased in order to allow generalization in the second step. Thirdly, the reduction was conducted by following the selection, bundling, construction and integration of the paraphrases. The categories were developed by relying on the inductive category development process.

3.2 Forms of embedded systems openness

As it came out in the second part of this thesis, the notion of ES openness which incorporates both a technical as well as an organizational perspective has not been elaborated in the literature. Therefore, one goal of this study was to find an integrated perspective on ES openness considering both technical as well as organizational factors.

The interview partners described three different forms of openness in the context of ES, which can be distinguished to the degree to which external actors are involved. The first form, which does not necessarily enable externals to participate, circulated around the implementation of common technical standards and the use of publicly available software. This could for example be the use of embedded Linux or Android on the operating systems layer, but also the use of open libraries or open standards. The motivation for this form of openness is not necessarily to involve externals, but there are other motivations as well. According to one interview partner: *"First of all, a proprietary ES has been built and then it has been realized, that something new is required and that there are already a lot of open approaches existing and it would not be profitable to build up these resources internally."* This approach towards openness is primarily motivated by reducing costs and compensating missing internal resources. As this approach can be implemented without the need to involve external participants, it can be conceptualized as internal openness.

In contrast to internal openness, the other approaches towards openness are motivated by involving externals and therefore can be clustered as external openness. Based on the data, there are two forms of external openness. There is the more traditional approach of involving externals based on a contract relationship: *"They would make an NDA and then some opening can occur. This is not that unusual."* This form of openness is not particularly new and already widely practiced, however, by implementing internal openness beforehand, the cooperation with external partners would be facilitated. To protect IP, this form of openness is often accompanied by contractual agreements like NDAs. As it is practiced with partners known to the firm, it can be conceptualized as network openness.

The second form of external openness is market openness. Market openness, in contrast to network openness, does not restrict potential external contributors to the ES, but external actors can themselves extend the ES without necessarily consulting the ES producer. Both forms of external openness, network and market openness, require defined external interfaces of the ES in order to change the system or build new applications on top of it, as one of the experts stated: *"By using defined interfaces, I do not see a problem for additional applications, as long as the interfaces are secure. However, I see a problem if it is possible to implement every kind of source code"*.

Another result of the interviews was that internal openness can be seen as a major facilitator for the two forms of external openness. However, internal openness does not necessarily lead to external openness, but can also be pursued by itself, as one interview partner stated: *"At the moment, we have a closed system based on an open platform, but we do not open it at the moment. When we open it, then we do it by involving the particular customer"*

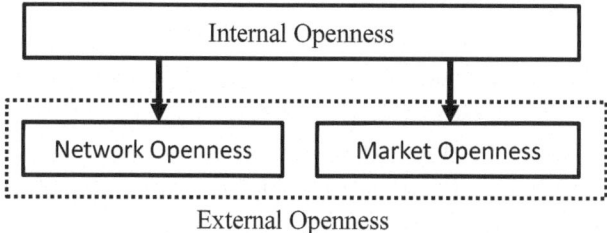

Figure 8   Forms of ES openness

The three forms of ES openness are depicted in Figure 8. These forms of openness have a similar focus as technological or platform openness. They also refer to the possibilities for external actors to participate in the development and commercialization of ES.

3.3   Technical factors influencing ES openness

From a technical point of view, the two most important influencing factors towards openness are safety and security. One expert stated: *"A common barrier is that ES are steering technical processes characterized by safety requirements. To balance between safety and*

openness is often difficult". To balance these different requirements, a common sugges-
tion was to divide the system into a critical and a non-critical part where only the non-
critical part should be subject to openness. As one interviewee put it: *"The current trend
is that the different [safety-/security-critical and non-safety/security-critical] functionalities have to be put together. And when you want to do that, you have to ensure strict
isolation"*. Real-time constraints are another technical characteristic of ES, which need
to be insured. When opening ES to externals, the ES producer needs to ensure, that new
applications made by third parties do not compromise these constraints.

One goal of internal openness, relying on open software platforms and standards is also
of particular importance to external openness strategies. These two foundations have
been explicitly named by a couple of interview partners, for instance: *"In my opinion,
standards are the key to success. And the opening of an existing ES solution does only
work, when there is some kind of open operating system on the ES"*. The establishment
of standards is also crucial to external openness as it attracts external actors: *"When a
standard or an open interface has reached a critical mass, some kind of community
emerges or a pool of experts from which a firm can benefit"*. Therefore the crucial role
of standards for the development of complementary applications as emphasized e.g. by
West (2003), Galvin (2008) or Grøtnes (2009) has been confirmed in the context of ES.
In particular, ES producers need to provide standardized interfaces to facilitate the development of new applications from external actors. Another requirement is a flexible
architecture, which is able to cope with a wide range of requirements. This can be addressed by implementing internal openness, as open platforms often provide more flexibility.

For many ES firms, ES openness is dependent on the availability of cheap, yet capable
hardware resources: *"For ES, every cent is important...every reduction of costs leads to
more potential for openness"*. For external openness, to incorporate external actors, documentation and in some cases also tool support is required to facilitate the development
of new applications.

Based on these results it can be seen that the technical factors can be categorized into
technical constraints and technical requirements of openness. Technical constraints determine the potential degree of openness, whereas technical requirements for openness
provide guidelines to realize ES openness. Some of the aspects like standardization have
already been explored in older literature, e.g. by Rashid et al. (1989), however, the goal
here is to collect all relevant aspects in the context of ES openness. The results of this
section have been depicted in Table 8 with the numbers showing how many interview

partners mentioned the particular aspect. From a technical point of view, both forms of external openness, network and market openness face the same constraints. However, when pursuing market openness, there is a higher risk of violating these constraints.

Table 8   The influence of technical factors on ES openness

	Technical constraints	Technical requirements
Internal openness	*No constraints found*	technical architecture (3); standardization (11); HW resources (4)
External openness	safety and security (10); RT-Constraints (5);	technical architecture (3); standardization (11); HW resources (4); connectivity (2); documentation and tool support (5); isolation (3)

3.4   Organizational factors influencing ES openness

One result of the data analysis was that the organizational factors influencing ES openness can be subdivided into internal and external organizational factors. Internal organizational factors refer to internal capabilities the organization needs to implement for openness. External organizational do not concern the internal organizational structure itself, but result from external requirements.

Internal organizational factors influencing ES openness

Internal openness with its focus on open platforms requires corresponding internal expertise, as one interviewee put it: *"with innovative applications in this sector, the complexity also rises, leading to more required know-how"*. As proprietary ES are more dedicated to designated functions, introducing open platforms would provide more flexibility. One interviewee stated: *"the employees and managers need to be able to deal with this kind of flexibility...and this flexibility also requires a broad body of knowledge"*. To increase flexibility and handle uncertainty, internal openness requires a stronger focus on communication and cooperation between the employees and less hierarchical relationships. One factor which has to be taken into account regarding the implementation of more organizational flexibility, is internal resistance. However, internal resistance constitutes a barrier to openness *"Especially the not-invented-here syndrome is one of the greatest barriers for people who have developed an ES in the last 15-20 years"*.

Due to the increased uncertainty and new ideas flowing in when involving externals, external openness requires a higher level of organizational flexibility. As one interview partner said: *"The potential, of course is that new ideas flow in. But at the same time, this is related with possible drawbacks: that you need innovative processes to handle the inflow of new ideas internally".* Therefore, ES firms need to be able to assimilate external knowledge and ideas. These capabilities of firms are especially addressed by literature on absorptive capacity, e.g. Cohen & Levinthal (1990). The field of absorptive capacity has been widely researched from different theoretical perspectives and has been informed by a great variety of empirical evidence (Volberda, Foss, and Lyles 2010). The role of absorptive capacity in the context of open innovation has e.g. been explored by Newey (2010). Furthermore, the cooperation with unknown external actors requires that these actors get support from the ES firms when developing new applications.

Another factor driving internal openness and network openness is to reduce costs. By reusing existing open software components, the complexity may rise, however, it is less costly than developing components such as an operating system or special libraries. Furthermore, when entering new markets, the risk of losing money is lower when involving external partners. One interviewee stated: *"When you want to enter in a new business sector where you do not have much experience, where the risk is too high, you would search for a partner to whom you would open your system."* However, in the case of network and market openness, the additional support requirements also lead to increasing costs.

Table 9 shows the internal organizational factors firms need to take care of regarding the different forms of ES openness. The second column shows the internal organizational factors relevant to a specific form of openness, whereas the third column shows the factors the three forms of openness have in common.

Table 9   The influence of internal organizational factors on ES openness

	Internal organizational factors	
Internal openness	possibility to reduce costs (5)	
Network openness	additional support requirements (3); possibility to reduce costs (5)	**Factors in common:** increase organizational flexibility (3); reduce internal resistance (4); required know-how (2)
Market openness	additional support requirements (3); ability to assimilate external knowledge and ideas (2); communication among technical staff and management (3)	

External organizational factors influencing ES openness

In the case of network and market openness, additional challenges arise due to legal requirements. Of particular importance are liability aspects. For some products, especially safety-critical products, ES firms need to certificate their systems whenever changes occur. One expert stated: *"There are a lot of certificated devices which are not allowed to be customized as they would lose their certification."* On the one hand, this increases safety when opening an ES. On the other hand, certification requirements often lead to additional overheads in terms of time and cost. Regarding market openness, the protection of IP is of particular importance. In contrast to network openness, where firms can protect their intellectual properties for instance by NDAs, such mechanisms are harder to enforce. Another important factor is user acceptance. With additional applications for an ES, the end users must be able to cope with the increasing product complexity. For instance, when considering application areas like smart home, the users might be overburdened by new functions. Another aspect is the field of data privacy.

For the success of market openness, the ability to control an ecosystem is a critical factor. This has been expressed by one of the experts: *"What you can see here, what Apple has demonstrated that the firm being in the center of an ecosystem earns most of the money."* For ES firms, according to this expert, one of the reasons why ES refrain from establishing an ecosystem is *"to realize where the ecosystem is located"*.

Summarizing, it can be said, that the experts have put particular emphasis on the legal aspects (IP protection and liability) when opening an ES to external participation. One interview partner stated: *"Regarding organizational factors...IP protection and liability are definitely the most important ones"*. The handling of these factors can decide between success and failure of ES openness: *"First of all, when a system gets opened, there is the risk, that certain safety aspects are not fulfilled anymore and I am responsible for the liability...and the other risk is that I loose intellectual property when I open my system too much"*. IP protection has been confirmed by most interview partners to be one of the most important factors ES firms need to consider when opening ES. To ensure IP protection, *"only the parts of a system will be opened which enable a broader utilization of these systems...for this reason, I would claim that the trend is towards closed systems with open interfaces"*. This seems to confirm the notion of IP modularity in the platforms literature, that ES firms implement modularity in their products by considering the criticality of their IP. In table 10, the results concerning the external organizational factors have been summarized.

Table 10   The influence of external organizational factors on ES openness

	External organizational factors
Internal openness	*(no external organizational factors according to the data)*
Network openness	certification requirements (6); liability (6)
Market openness	certification requirements (6); liability (6); IP protection (7); data privacy (2); user acceptance (1); control of the ecosystem (2); product life span (2)

3.5   Discussion

The study presents three different forms of openness ES firms can pursue when conduction open innovation. They describe to what degree firms should open themselves to external partners depending on the associated technical and organizational risk and challenges. Although the notion that firms should take openness decisions in accordance with certain factors like IP protection is not completely new, the present study provides additional insights. First of all, the challenges of ES are not present in other kinds of systems but their consideration is crucial for OI in ES. The results show, that firms have to pursue an integrated approach both considering organizational as well as technical factors for their OI strategy. A particular strategy that was discovered in the study is the pursuit of internal openness. This allows firms to take a gradual approach towards open innovation, while at the same time also benefitting their own capability to innovate.

3.6   Conclusion

The aim of this study was to explore how ES firms can pursue the opening of their embedded systems and their organization in order to enable open innovation. Through expert interviews, the study has shown that ES firms have to master technical, internal and external organizational challenges when opening their systems. Regarding ES openness, a conceptualization has been provided, which categorizes different types of openness, namely internal, network and market openness. Furthermore, internal openness greatly facilitates network and market openness. When pursuing internal openness, the primary objective is not to enable open innovation, but other motivations like saving costs or introducing a stable technical architecture are the main reasons. To implement internal openness, firms would need to move towards open platforms and standardization. In addition, organizational challenges like internal resistance have to be overcome. When pursuing external openness, technical characteristics like safety and security are especially significant due to the threat of violation by external applications. Therefore, from a technical point of view, openness is largely determined by the degree to which the isolation of safety- and security-critical parts can be ensured. In addition to the technical factors, ES openness is also strongly influenced by external organizational factors, mainly legal issues like IP protection and liability aspects.

This study has several limitations. Due to the broad application areas of embedded systems with a broad set of different requirements and in regard to the limited data base, the results of the interview study can only be generalized to a limited degree. Therefore, further research would be needed to provide a deeper insight into different fields of embedded systems. This study can be seen as a first step towards researching the notion of openness in the field of ES. The different facets of openness could also be investigated more thoroughly, especially concerning the lessening of restrictions on use, development and commercialization of ES. Furthermore, the results do not yet consider openness on a modular level. As it has been seen, partial openness can be achieved by opening particular modules. Especially the influence of critical factors like IP protection or liability on potential openness would be of interest. Besides legal aspects, further research on the cost aspects of ES openness would also be required. From a technical point of view, another research question would be to explore the influence of openness on the architecture of ES. This study shows relevant factors regarding ES openness, but the degree to which these factors are crucial for the decision towards openness and how they influence firms' decisions in pursuing ES openness still needs to be further explored. Opening ES also challenges existing business models. In particular, by opening ES, firms have to shift their focus on managing the ecosystem of firms emerging by opening their systems.

4   Study 3 – Technical opening of embedded systems for open innovation[4]

As it has been laid out in chapter 1 of this part, the following study deals with potential forms of modularization of ES to enable open innovation. It aims to answer the research question *"How can embedded systems be modularized to enable open innovation?"*. The study builds in particular on the theoretical foundations on modularity which have been presented in chapter II.4.5. The study is structured in the following way: First of all, the

---

[4] An earlier version of this chapter was presented at the *19th Pacific Asia Conference on Information Systems (PACIS 2015)*, Singapore (2015) and published as (Soeldner, Roth, and Moeslein 2015).

research design of the study is presented, detailing the data collection process (4.1.1) and the conducted data analysis (4.1.2). In the subsequent section (4.2) the individual cases are described, followed by the cross-case analysis (4.3). After the results have been analyzed, section 4.4 provides a discussion of key findings and section 4.5 presents the conclusion of the study.

4.1 Research design

To answer the research question, how ES can be technically opened to enable open innovation, a multiple-case design was chosen. According to Yin (2008), case studies are used to explore a phenomenon in depth in the context in which it occurs and where the boundaries between phenomenon and context cannot be clearly determined. To account for the complexity in the context of ES, multiple case studies have been conducted. This allowed us to cover a broad range of different ES. The following chapter describes the data collection and the data analysis process conducted for this study.

4.1.1 Data collection

The study relies on multiple cases in order to follow a replication logic which allows to extract generalizable patterns but also to find contradictory evidence in the other cases (Eisenhardt 1989; Yin 2008). The cases itself have been selected according to the guidelines laid out by Eisenhardt & Graebner (2007), which state that the sample selection should be performed by choosing cases which are particularly suitable for uncovering and extending relationships and logic among constructs. To allow generalizability, cases where selected to reflect a broad variety of embedded systems.

Case selection was guided by the following requirements:

- The cases should cover a broad variety of different ES from different industries, which increases the possibility to generalize the results.
- The cases should both include ES with different degrees of openness. This ranges from mere data access to the possibility to change the ES itself both on the software as well as on the hardware layer.
- The cases should include ES with different degrees of designation to particular use cases. This means, that both 'traditional' ES which are mainly developed for

a particular purposes as well as ES whose use cases are not clearly designated by the ES producer, are included. Therefore, also ES, which represent ES platforms, have been included. These platforms do not specify any particular use case but allow the users to determine the purpose of the system itself. In these cases, to allow open innovation would be the primary purpose of these platforms.

- The cases included should also feature ES with different levels of dependability and RT requirements. As it has been shown, these characteristics can often be considered as constraints towards openness. Including cases, which are subjects to these requirements to a higher degree, allows to show the influence of these requirements on openness.

In total, 16 cases with 13 being commercial industry examples were selected, and three cases, which are based on, research projects focusing on openness for third-party enhancements. This allows to not only include current developments in industry, but also to include developments not yet implemented in practice. Although the cases span across different industries, the author believes that this strengthens the findings as it allows covering ES which are subject to different degrees of safety & security requirements and RT-constraints. Data acquisition took place between July 2013 and January 2014.

After identification of the cases, the organizations were contacted in order to conduct an interview with either the corresponding project manager or an employee with in-depth knowledge about the technical aspects respectively the strategy concerning openness of their ES. The interview was conducted by using a semi-structured interview guideline, which was development base on theoretical findings in the literature. In total interviews were conducted with 9 out of 16 of the organizations participating in the study. Although the other cases do not include an interview, there was circumstantial documentation available, which allowed to include these cases. Especially the ES platform cases were richly documented as they target a wide variety of users and often also have a viable community. In addition, different kinds of written material which was available publicly from the companies' website and from other external sources have been collected, e.g. from press articles, professional journal as well as research papers. Thus, more insights regarding the motivations of openness, the factors influencing design decisions as well as more details on the modularity of the opened ES, was gained. Table 11 gives an overview about the cases as well as the respective industries, about the used sources used the interview partners.

The following cases represent 'classical' ES where openness is enable to spur additional use cases, but which do not change the core designation of the system:

INCA, Infotainment case, John Deere, Kuka Youbot, OpenXC, Commercial Vehicle Case. Due to reasons of confidentiality, the cases will be referred to by their industry name (e.g. Infotainment Case and Commercial Vehicle Case).

The following cases deal with ES which can be seen as generic platform targeting a specific industry: AutoPNP, Prosyst, Qivicon and RACE.

The following cases fall under the ES platforms category which do not target any specific industry: Raspberry PI, Arduino, Google Glass, Google Project ARA, SmartThings as well as LEGO Mindstorms. I included only ES platforms, which deliver all the necessary means to build a product out of it and are intended to be used as a toolkit to build ES. This was done in order to exclude component producers, which can be used as one part to build an ES, but do not itself constitute an ES platform. In contrast to classical ES, they often also target non-expert users who do not necessarily have a background in ES development, thus broadening potential contributors to the ES platform. As these platforms are especially dedicated towards open innovation, they provide additional insights.

Table 11   Cases overview

Case	Industry	Sources used for the cases	Position of Interviewee
AutoPNP: SW architecture for automation systems	Research institution / Automation	Interview; Documentation	Project leader
INCA: open camera platform by Fraunhofer Institute	Research institution / Camera industry	Interview; Documentation	Project leader
Infotainment Platform: automotive infotainment platform	Automotive	Interview	Department manager, project leader
John Deere: agricultural vehicles	Commercial vehicles	Interview; Documentation	Advanced engineer
Kuka Youbot: prototyping robotics systems for research and education	Robotics	Interview; Documentation	Product manager
Prosyst E-Health Middleware for e-health platforms	ES engineering; E-Health	Interview; Documentation; Presentations	Technology evangelist
Qivicon: smart-home platform	Telecommunications	Interview; Documentation	Product owner
OpenXC: open-source platform to develop vehicle-data based applications	Automotive / Infotainment	Documentation; Website	

RACE Project: decentralized ICT architecture for cars	Research project by firm consortium / Automotive	Interview; Documentation; Research paper; Press releases	Project leader
Commercial vehicle platform: platform for data-based SW applications for commercial vehicles	ES engineering / Commercial vehicles	Interview; Documentation	Business unit manager
Raspberry PI: programmable mini computer usable for ES	Industry agnostic ES platform	Website; Documentation; Press articles	
Arduino: ES platform based on a wide range of ES components	Industry agnostic ES platform	Website; Documentation; Press articles	
Google Glass: wearable computing platform	Industry agnostic ES platform	Website; Documentation; Press articles	
Project Ara: hardware-modular smart phone	Smart phone platform	Website; Documentation; Press articles	
SmartThings: open platform for smart homes	Home automation platform	Website; Documentation; Press articles	
LEGO Mindstorms: programmable robotic platform for education	Robotics platform for children	Website; Documentation; Press articles	

4.1.2 Data analysis

For data analysis, the sources named in Table 11 have been used. As some cases did not include interviews, firstly the data analysis process for the cases with interviews will be described, and secondly the cases which were elicited without interviews.

Each of the recorded interviews has been transcribed verbatim. In the next step, the coding of the data was achieved by applying template analysis (King 1998). The codes were based both on the literature as well as on the underlying research question (Coffey and Atkinson 1996). The main hierarchical categories were based on the literature on modularity, openness, open innovation and embedded systems which also provided a starting set of subcategories. Coding of data has been accomplished independently by two parties with the help of the qualitative research software MaxQDA. After initial coding, the data has been compared with the existing material by following an analyst triangulation process (Yin 2008). For triangulation, different sources have been used as depicted in Table

11. Some of the additional documentation was supplied by the interview partners themselves and gave additional insights into the specific ES, its architecture and openness. In other cases publicly available technical documents have been consulted which detailed certain technical standards or specifications. This also included material from standardization organizations relevant for the cases. Company websites have been another source of documentation. Often the documentation available on the websites targeted external developers and therefore provided technical details as well as insights in the openness of the ES. A complete overview of the publicly available websites used in this study can be found in Annex A. Similarly to the interview transcripts, the additional documentation was also coded. Coding was done by two independent researchers. If data collected from the various sources were inconsistent or contradictory, the author went back to the interviewee to clarify issues.

To code the non-interview data, the following procedure has been conducted: The written sources have been systematically examined. Relevant text passages have been extracted and subsequently paraphrased. Based on that, also additional codes emerged.

Broadly, the focus in the analysis was on the following themes: the form and degree of openness chosen by the ES provider and the modular design of the systems to enable open innovation. In the first step, the systems have been analyzed regarding the forms of openness they offer to externals. Based on that, the implications of openness on the modularity of the system has been explored by applying the main design principles of modularity. The focus was on the factors affecting the openness of a system and how the modularization of a system can help to facilitate open innovation while minimizing technical and organizational risks. This allowed gaining a clearer picture how openness is implemented by modularizing the system accordingly. During this process, the aims and use cases firms pursue by opening their systems were considered. The data of the different cases has been compared by a cross-case analysis which enhances the generalizability of case results, but also helps to gain a better understanding of the phenomenon (Miles, Huberman, and Saldana 2013; Yin 2008). This allowed to draw general conclusions moving from specific cases of ES openness to a comprehensive view of ES openness and its required forms of modularization.

The analysis of the modular implications of openness was driven by applying modularity theory according to Baldwin & Clark (2000) with a focus on the design rules concept. In addition, the principles of abstraction, information hiding and partitioning as well as standardization of interfaces were used to analyze the impact of openness on the modularity of ES. These principles were used to describe how ES firms implement openness in their systems and the impact of the openness on the modular structure of their systems. In the case descriptions, I consolidated these modular design principles to three main classes: *Architecture and Partitioning, Abstraction* and *Interfaces*. For each case, it has been described how the cases were making use of these modular principles in order to implement openness respectively open innovation.

4.2 Cases

4.2.1 Raspberry PI

Case introduction

Raspberry Pi is a low-cost computer in the dimension of a conventional credit card. It was developed by the Raspberry Pi foundation, a charity organization whose primary mission is to teach children around the world programming. One of their key requirements to the platform is that the devices must be affordable and at the same time able to run a modern operating system. At the time of writing, the company offers two variations of the mini-computer; model a sells for $25 with 256 MB RAM, one USB port and no Ethernet whereas the slightly better and higher priced $35 model b has 512 MB RAM, two USB ports and Ethernet, respectively[5]

The Raspberry Pi itself does not necessarily represent an embedded system, as it is based on general-purpose computer components without providing sensors and actuators, but it provides the basic building blocks, which can be combined to create embedded systems. To some degree, it has more communalities to a normal PC (Wallace and Richardson 2012)

Since June 2014, Raspberry Pi also released a smaller version of the Raspberry PI, the "Raspberry Pi Compute Module"[6]. In essence, the Compute Module is a smaller version of the Raspberry Pi without key interfaces like LAN, USB etc. Instead, the Compute Module can be plugged into an own printed circuit board (PCB), which can be designed by the users itself and allows the users to extend the hardware base. In addition, the Raspberry Pi offers the "Compute Module IO Board", which provides key interfaces the Compute Module is missing. This helper module itself is open hardware, therefore allowing users to come up with their own version.

---

[5] See https://www.raspberrypi.org/help/faqs/#introWhatIs; retrieved September 2014
[6] See http://www.raspberrypi.org/raspberry-pi-compute-module-new-product/; retrieved September 2014

Partitioning

In its original form, the Raspberry Pi is delivered as a SoC. Therefore, it consists of a single module encompassing all subcomponents, which make up the whole platform.7 Thus, the partitioning of the Raspberry Pi platform is rather integral on its lower hardware layer. The Raspberry Pi itself only offers a limited number of additional hardware modules extending the functionality, e.g. an additional camera board. The components residing on the Raspberry Pi board cannot be changed, constituting the core part of the platform.

This way of portioning may not constrain the range of possible application which can be realized with the Raspberry Pi, but for many tasks, a simpler hardware platform like Arduino could be more suitable (Wallace and Richardson 2012), especially for use cases where the requirements to the hardware platforms are not too high.

The original strategy of partitioning the whole system on a single printed circuit board has changed with the introduction of the Compute Module in combination with the Compute Module IO Board[8]. This repartitioning allows the users to still rely on the core components of a Raspberry Pi (the Compute Module), while at the same time enabling open innovation at the level of the Compute Module IO Board. This partitioning reflects their openness strategy. While the core parts are still closed (the CPU, RAM as well as the flash memory) and cannot be opened due to being based on proprietary components, the Compute Module IO Board represents the open part changeable by the user.

Figure 9   Compute module IO board / Compute module (Image source: raspberrypi.org)

---

[7] See https://www.raspberrypi.org/help/faqs/#generalSoCUsed; retrieved September 2014
[8] See http://www.raspberrypi.org/raspberry-pi-compute-module-new-product/; retrieved September 2014

Figure 9 shows both the Computer Module IO Board (left side) as well as the Compute Module IO Board in combination with the Computer module (right side).

Interfaces

Although the core Raspberry Pi board itself cannot be changed by the users, it offers a variety of standardized interfaces allowing to plug additional components or to make the Raspberry Pi a part of a larger system. Although the Raspberry Pi board itself is rather monolithic, by using these interfaces, users can extend the system with additional hardware components, which implement these standards. The General Purpose Input Output (GPIO) interface is particularly useful to connect all kinds of sensors or actuators (Wallace and Richardson 2012), hence allowing for a wide range of different modules to be integrated with the Raspberry Pi. They can be used both to sending a signal to another device as well as receiving signals from other devices (Arduino GPIO). This allows for instance to use external sensors with the Raspberry Pi and process incoming data, but also to use external actuators.

Abstraction

As the Raspberry PI constitutes a general-purpose platform with similar capabilities than previous generations of PCs, it also features the standardized composition in a hardware, software, and application layer. Additional particularities regarding the use of the abstraction principle have not been found in this case.

Encountered forms of openness

The Raspberry Pi is open to new hardware components, as it provides standardized interfaces which allow connecting all kinds of modules which just have to conform to the particular standard. However, the original hardware base itself is not opened for externals. With the introduction of the "Compute Module" and the "Compute Module IO Board", Raspberry Pi could release part of their base as open source, while at the same time protecting proprietary parts. According to James Adams, Director of Hardware of the Raspberry PI foundation, Raspberry Pi's strategy behind the Compute Module is to react to the growing number of users, which embed the Raspberry Pi in their system or their commercial products[9]. In essence, Raspberry PI follows a mixed source strategy, combining both proprietary as well as open hardware components.

On the software layer, the Raspberry PI rests on the Raspbian operating systems which is a based on of Debian Linux, thus being open source, although other operating systems

---

[9] See http://makezine.com/2014/04/07/new-raspberry-pi-compute-module-unveiled/; retrieved September 20014

are also supported (Wallace and Richardson 2012). Thus, developers can install any application supported by the hardware.

Degree of openness

The last section has shown that the Raspberry Pi is completely open on the software layer. On the hardware layer, it allows to integrate various modules with the Raspberry Pi by providing a set of standardized interfaces. However, at least with the original Raspberry Pi, it is not possible to change the main hardware module, due to the proprietary status of the SoC. As the preceding section has shown, Raspberry Pi also released a remodularized version also allowing to partly change the core HW components of a Raspberry Pi.

4.2.2 Arduino

Case introduction

The aim of the Arduino platform is to provide a tool for the creation of computers, which are able to sense and control the physical environment to a larger degree then a normal desktop computer. The core platform consists of an open-source physical computing environment consisting of a simple microcontroller board, a development environment supporting software development for the board and a wide range of additional components, so-called shields[10]

The range of products which can be developed by using the Arduino platform is rather broad: basically, the solution space is largely defined by the number of available sensors and actuators or other types of shields. In addition, due to the open hardware strategy, additional hardware components can be developed by the users themselves or existing Arduino hardware components can be changed. Regarding software, Arduino relies on open source software, therefore allowing the users to adjust the software to their needs[11]. Therefore, new products based on Arduino can either be created by recombining existing modules, by changing or by the creation of new modules.

The enhancement of the system by additional hardware and software parts is supported by its modularization. The modularization itself revolves around particular sensors and actuators and are realized as 'shields', which can be connected to the base board. Examples for such shields are for instance a dedicated Ethernet Shield, a Wi-Fi Shield or a Motor Shield. In addition, users can also connect accessories like a TFT LCD screen, or

---

[10] See http://arduino.cc/en/Guide/Introduction; retrieved September 2014
[11] See http://arduino.cc/en/Main/FAQ; retrieved September 2014

a USB adapter[12]. Due to the open hardware strategy used by Arduino, users can not only innovate outside existing module boundaries, but each module can be adjusted itself.

Partitioning

The analysis of its architecture has shown, that Arduino is largely modularized according to functions, thus allowing to change each function independently of the rest of the system. The modularization of the Arduino platform is aligned around functions, usually with one core function per hardware component. Arduino distinguishes between boards, shields, kits and accessories[13]. The boards feature a programmable microcontroller and provide interfaces used to connect other devices and components. The shields are offering additional functionality, e.g. a display shield, USB shield etc. Thus, Arduino's approach towards partitioning also reflects general-purpose platforms.

Standardization and interfaces

The Arduino platform shows a particular emphasis on standardization, allowing to easily extend the platform with additional hardware modules. However, for the creation of new Arduino hardware components, certain design rules need to be followed. First of all, Arduino components have standardized physical interfaces allowing the different components to be 'stacked', which is realized by standardized hardware interfaces based on stacking headers. This allows combining a theoretically unlimited number of shields, similarly to LEGO bricks[14]

Arduino thus created one particular hardware interface standard, which allows combining a broad variety of different modules. From the perspective of external innovators, this facilitates the creation of new modules, as they do not need to handle various kinds of interface standards. Thus, the modularization of the Arduino platform is similar to LEGO bricks, as one shield usually offers one overall function with each shield offering the same interface standard.

In addition, Arduino also offers a broad variety of standardized interfaces, like USB etc., thus enabling users to integrate non-Arduino devices in their solution. Additional interfaces can also be implemented by externals via additional shields.

Abstraction

Another modularization principle Arduino relies on to facilitate open innovation is to abstract the inner details of microcontroller programming. Normally, this would require

---

[12] https://hci.rwth-aachen.de/tiki-download_wiki_attachment.php?attId=2292; Retrieved September 2014
[13] http://arduino.cc/en/Main/Products; Retrieved September 2014
[14] http://www.freetronics.com/pages/stacking-arduino-shields; Retrieved September 2014

the users to have detailed technical understanding[15]. To facilitate software development, the Arduino platform offers certain software libraries, e.g. Wiring, which abstract the hardware details for the users. The use of certain libraries and frameworks is common to hide complexity from developers. Although this approach is widespread in designing computer systems, it has not been so widespread for hardware platforms and microcontroller development. At the same time, experienced users can expand the Arduino language by using C++ libraries.

Software development for the Arduino is facilitated by the Arduino Integrated Development Environment (IDE), which is part of the platform. Arduino programs are called 'sketches' which are developed using the IDE and then uploaded to the Arduino board for execution. Due to the abstraction of the complexities of development with hardware, users do not need to have in-depth expertise in embedded systems development.

Encountered forms of openness

The Arduino platform features multiple forms of openness both on the hardware as well on the software layer. In particular, it tries to stimulate hardware developments by externals. Due to the release of Arduino under a Creative Common License (CCL), the platform as a whole can be improved and changed by externals. Thus, it cannot not only be enhanced by additional modules, but existing boards and shields can be modified as well. As the Arduino is based on Atmel's ATMEGA8 and ATMEGA168 microcontrollers, whose modules are published under a Creative Common license, users have the permission of building their own versions of Arduino, allowing the creation both of personal as well as commercial derivatives. In addition to the open hardware status of Arduino, many users freely reveal software they have written for the Arduino, which can be found at the Arduino "Playground"[16]. Openness is further enhanced by the availability of documentation. Ranging from tutorials, code examples, instructions and sample projects, external innovators can benefit from the community revolving around Arduino. Thus, the Arduino platform is steadily enhanced by users, further facilitating open innovation.

Degree of openness

Due to its open hardware as well as open source status, Arduino aims to increase adoption by third parties, with less regard to potential revenue due to sales. External companies can produce the official boards by paying a license fee to the Arduino team for the further development of the project[17]. Arduino also does not follow a service business model

---

[15] http://arduino.cc/en/Guide/Introduction; Retrieved September 2014
[16] See http://playground.arduino.cc/; Retrieved September 2014
[17] See http://arduino.cc/en/Main/FAQ; Retrieved September 2014

providing support or additional services to users against payment, which is often found in open source business models. With the current level of openness, such a business model can also not be defended easily against competitors, as the whole design information of the Arduino platform is revealed.

Although there has been a variety of clones of Arduino hardware emerging[18], Arduino maintains a list of official Arduino hardware components, which can be seen as a 'soft' level of control. This type of control is not based on contractual regulations but on user's perceptions regarding quality and trust. However, at the time of writing, the founders argue about the future status of Arduino as an open platform[19]. Whereas some of the founders aim to continue Arduino as an open platform, an increasing number of Arduino microcontrollers are produced by externals. Although it is part of the Arduino mission to promote externals producing Arduino clones, an increasing risk is seen in the counterfeit of the Arduino logo, as some producers are illegally selling Arduino clones as hardware originally produced by Arduino.

In comparison to the other cases, Arduino is farthest on the degree of openness. Due to its open hardware and open source status, externals are allowed to make changes to all of its hardware and software base. The main goal is not the maximization of profits, but rather to maximize the adoption of the platform. As Arduino modules can be produced by everybody who holds the required capacity, it cannot be guaranteed, that Arduino earns its share for every Arduino sold. Still, Arduino holds some control over its platform, with Arduino releasing new versions of its main modules regularly. Furthermore, Arduino also holds a list of approved Arduino models, which acts similarly as a certification. Due to Arduinos prices, which are close to the costs of production, openness in this case does not necessarily give rise to competition. An interesting direction for future research would be how to build sustainable business models on top of a platform like Arduino.

4.2.3 Google Glass

Case introduction

Google Glass is a computer in the form of eye glasses encompassing a small screen, a camera, a speaker, a microphone as well as GPS. Google lists a variety of use cases

---

[18] See http://arstechnica.com/information-technology/2013/10/arduino-creator-explains-why-open-source-matters-in-hardware-too, Retrieved February 2015
[19] See http://www.heise.de/newsticker/meldung/Arduino-gegen-Arduino-Gruender-streiten-um-die-Firma-2549653.html; Retrieved February 2015

ranging from Search, Navigation, Mail and Calendar, "Now Cards", Phone Calls and SMS, to photos, videos and video calls[20]. Next to these use cases, Google Glass offers APIs and software development tools for externals to broaden the range of applications. Concerning its hardware base, Google Glass has similar characteristics as smart phones[21]. Technically, it houses a TI OMAP4430 processor, 16GB SanDisk flash memory, as well as an Elpida mobile DRAM chip[22]. The operating system running on top of it is Google Android, an OS with which a high number of app developers are already familiar. Therefore, Google Glass offers many functions already known from smart phones, but due to its status as a wearable device, enables additional application areas. As user interaction occurs in a hands-free fashion, it allows usage in different contexts not covered by smart phones.

Similarly to smart phones, the use of Google Glass rests to a high degree on the apps which are offered for it. Besides the use of Google Glass in the private domain, there is a broad potential for use cases in professional fields such as construction, in medicine or in the military[23].

Partitioning

The partitioning of its hardware components is to a large degree determined by its design as a wearable device. Therefore, the form factor requiring Google Glass both being unobtrusive but at the same time fashionable determines the modularization of the device to a large degree. The arrangement of the different components follows these considerations. For the partitioning of third-party applications on the hardware, developers can choose between two fundamental models. Applications can either be executed directly on the device by using the Glass Development Kit (GDK) or by making use of the "Mirror API", which allows building web-based services running in the cloud[24]. From an openness perspective, this unlocks a wider range of applications, as they can make use of additional hardware capabilities, which are otherwise limited by the device itself. Furthermore, the Mirror API also offers platform independence, as there is no restriction which programming language or platform to use for the web-based services. To integrate certain external devices, Google provides the MyGlass App. One use case is to get location data from another device, which has the MyGlass App installed.

---

[20] See https://support.google.com/glass/answer/3064131?hl=en; Retrieved October 2014
[21] See http://www.pcmag.com/article2/0,2817,2416488,00.asp; Retrieved October 2014
[22] See http://www.techinsights.com/teardown.com/google-glass/; Retrieved October2014

[23] See http://www.forbes.com/sites/quora/2012/07/06/what-could-be-interesting-use-cases-for-google-glass/3/ Retrieved October 2014
[24] For more details, see https://developers.google.com/glass/; Retrieved October 2014

Interfaces and standardization

As an operating system, Google Glass uses Android, which is the most widely used operating system for smart phones at the time of writing, but also gaining ground on other types of devices. Although the use of Android as an OS is obvious, as it is also developed by Google, Android with its large community of developers is a de-facto standard for app developers. In addition, Google offers two different interfaces for third-party software development. As described in the last section, the two primary interfaces for external developers are the GDK and the Mirror API. These two interfaces reflect two different approaches. Whereas the Mirror API allows the integration of cloud-based web services, applications built with the GDK on the other hand allow low-level access to the hardware components. Other advantages of the GDK is the offline functionality and to allow real-time user interaction[25].

A particularly important API for developing with Google Glass is the Mirror API, which for instance allows to incorporate external web services. This mirror API also enables Google Glass to become part of a larger system.

Abstraction

Google Glass uses abstraction mechanisms to hide the complexity of the underlying platform from its third-party developers and therefore facilitate development. In addition to the standard Android SDK, as previously mentioned, Glass offers the Mirror API as well as the GDK as tools for apps development. As apps for Glass are rather specific due to the specific requirements regarding user interaction, Glass also offers "patterns" which guide the developer when realizing certain design aspects. These patterns constitute a further layer, which guides the development of the user interactions elements. These patterns abstract the single user interface elements in common patterns, which can be used as templates when designing the user interface. Examples for such patterns are the "Static card", the "Live card", "Periodic Notifications" or the "Immersion" pattern[26]. The use of these patterns also facilitates development, as the developer does not have to figure out by himself how to implement common user interface elements.

Encountered forms of openness

The degree of openness of Google Glass is similar to smart phones, granting third-party developers the possibility to develop additional software applications while retaining the

---

[25] See https://developers.google.com/glass/develop/gdk/; Retrieved October 2014
[26] See https://developers.google.com/glass/design/patterns; Retrieved October 2014

hardware base closed. Regarding openness for software, Google Glass provides developer tools facilitating the development of additional applications. Additional applications mainly revolve around the innovative use of Google Glass' sensors. Google Glass itself does not prescribe any particular use cases, with Google Glass exhibiting characteristics of a general-purpose system on the software layer. From a hardware perspective, Google Glass is rather closed, as the existing hardware base cannot be changed. Regarding its hardware components, Google Glass is monolithic. An additional scenario for openness arises due to Google Glass' capability to be integrated in the cloud. Google Glass developers can develop software in the cloud which can access one (or more) Google Glass devices.

Degree of openness

The utility Google Glass offers is dependent on the applications, which are running on top of it. Although it is not yet clear at the time of writing how many applications Google itself will offer, the utility increases with the number of external applications. Google Glass apps, so-called Glassware is centrally provided via its app store *Google Play*. Concerning openness and the value offered by Google and by externals, Google Glass offers many similarities to the strategy Google employs in the smart phone domain. The app store allows both externals and Google to capture profits through the sales of additional apps. Opening in the case of Google Glass not only involves opening the underlying embedded system, but also entails partially opening the distribution channel. The opening of the distribution channel involves granting access to externals to market their applications via the app marketplace.

4.2.4 Project Ara

Case introduction

Project Ara is a project, which aims at creating a modular hardware ecosystem in the mobile phone domain. It is conducted by Google's Advanced Technology and Projects (ATAP) group. However, at the time of writing, ARA is yet a development project of Google which is to be released as a market pilot in 2015. Although Project Ara has not yet been commercialized, it has been included as a case in this thesis, because it allows analyzing how hardware modularity could be implemented in an industry characterized by a high level of integral design of its hardware components. In contrast to existing mobile phone platforms, Project Ara builds on a modular hardware platform enabling users to come up with so-called blocks. These blocks are standardized hardware components, which can be added to the Project Ara phone. Therefore, they allow users to customize their own smart phones. The customization thus goes beyond aesthetic changes, such as changing the cover of the smart phone, but also to customize the functionalities of the smart phone. Next to the possibility to customize the phone with additional modules, it also allows to easily replace broken parts, such limiting the time and effort for repair. In addition, the hardware base of the phone can thus be upgraded which is not yet possible with current generations of smart phones[27].

The platform itself consists of an endoskeleton, which represents the structural frame and the data backbone of the device. It is equipped with networking functionality for the modules and a back-up battery[28]. This frame can then be enhanced with modules enhancing the device's functionality. These modules can also be removed while the phone is powered on. Similar to the app store concept, additional modules can be acquired at the Ara Module Marketplace. On the software layer, Project Ara is using Google's Android operating system, which allows to integrate the already large ecosystem around that software platform[29].

Similar to the already existing ecosystem of external developers in the software field, Project Ara aims to create an ecosystem in the hardware domain. This vision was stated by Paul Eremenko who is the head of Project Ara: "We believe that the smartphone hardware ecosystem should be, and can be, a lot more like the Android app ecosystem: with a low barrier to entry, lots and lots of developers, and faster, richer innovation"[30].

Partitioning

From a modularity perspective, hardware modularity for smart phones poses a particular challenge. According to Ara Knaian, lead mechanical engineer on Project Ara: "A big challenge on this project was that a cell phone is one of the most integrated things that's made today, and we're trying to separate it into modular pieces." One reason for the strong integrality of smart phones is to keep its size and its weight small[31].

The partitioning follows a core-periphery logic. As already described, Google provides an endoskeleton. It possesses eight rear slots for modules and two front-facing slots, which can for instance be used for a screen and a button panel. Figure 10 shows a schematic depiction of Google Ara's architecture. In addition, the frame features an onboard

---

[27] See http://www.projectara.com/faq/; Retrieved October 2014
[28] See http://time.com/10115/google-project-ara-modular-smartphone/; Retrieved October 2014
[29] See http://www.projectara.com/faq; Retrieved October 2014
[30] See http://www.technologyreview.com/news/525386/why-googles-modular-smartphone-might-actually-succeed/; Retrieved October 2014
[31] See http://time.com/10115/google-project-ara-modular-smartphone/; Retrieved October 2014

power and data transmission[32].Thus, Google would control the primary interface standard for the modules provided by partners. A particular module does not necessarily possess only one function, but can support a variety of functions as well.

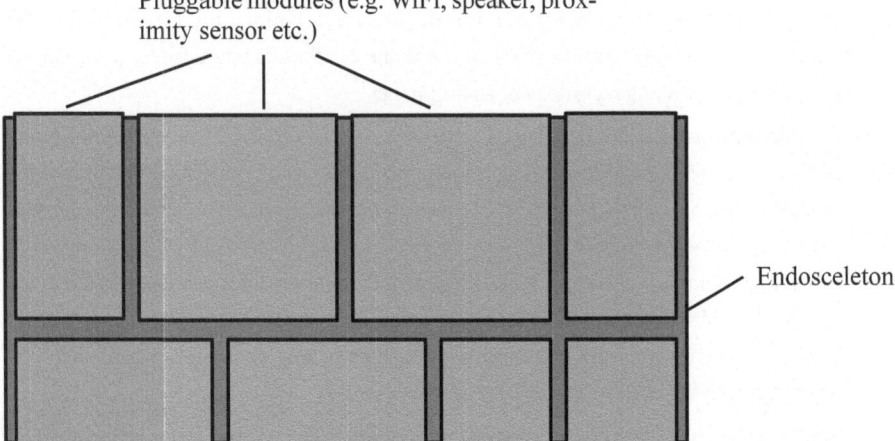

Figure 10 Schematic depiction of Google Ara's architecture

The biggest challenge for Project Ara is to achieve similar performance characteristics
with a modular architecture than traditional smart phone architecture, which are usually
highly integrative at the hardware layer. To allow externals to contribute with hardware
modules, Project Ara prescribes the design of external modules. External modules thus
have to conform to the design rules of Project Ara regarding size and interface standards.

Interfaces

The regular changing of the modules also puts a challenge on the interfaces due to the
mechanical abrasions on the interfaces, which would make them unreliable. Therefore,
Project Ara is relying on a particular interface standard ("capacitive interconnects")
which are wireless and should thus increase reliability but also save space. The modules
itself are connected to the frame via an electropermanent magnet which facilitates swap-
ping modules[33].

Abstraction

---

[32] See   http://www.technologyreview.com/news/525386/why-googles-modular-smartphone-might-actually-suc-
ceed/; Retrieved October 2014
[33]   See   http://www.theverge.com/2014/4/15/5615880/building-blocks-how-project-ara-is-reinventing-the-
smartphone; Retrieved October 2014

An important embodiment of abstraction in Project Ara is the module development kit. The development of hardware puts the designer in front of additional challenges not encountered in software development, such as manufacturing the hardware modules itself. A common trend in embedded system development is to try to develop as much as possible of the hardware components via software tools before they have to be actually manufactured. The module development kit (MDK) aims to allow manufacturers to test and prototype their hardware modules purely in software[34] . Furthermore it also provides reference implementation for various design features. Although the MDK can be categorized as tooling, it abstracts complexity of the development process of new modules.

Encountered Forms of Openness

The main objective of openness on the Project Ara platform is to spur the development of modular hardware components by externals. The approach towards openness reflects the software openness which is already been found in current smart phones. Whereas current smart phones have a fixed set of sensors and hardware capabilities, Project Ara aims to revolutionize smart phones by choosing a modular hardware design.

Degree of openness

On the hardware layer, Project Ara exhibits a closed core / open periphery architecture. Externally developed hardware modules are planned to be sold via a marketplace similar to its app store Google Play for its Android operating system. Thus, Project Ara also controls the distribution channel, which would allow them to generate additional earnings via the marketplace. Another advantage of such a centralized distribution channel is that it allows testing and certifying externally developed modules.

4.2.5   SmartThings

Case introduction

SmartThings is an open smart home platform allowing consumers to control all kinds of domestic appliances via a single app. In August 2014, Samsung acquired it for about $200 million[35]. The most important application areas are climate control, security, music and lighting. It allows the consumer to steer the integrated devices via a smart phone[36]. Some basic additional modules are provided by SmartThings themselves in order to provide a viable platform which already offers utility without complementary enhancements

---

[34] See http://www.wired.com/2014/10/day-with-project-ara/; Retrieved October 2014

[35] See http://time.com/3117493/samsung-home-automation-smartthings/; Retrieved October 2014

[36] See http://thenextweb.com/insider/2014/05/21/smartthings-officially-launches-connected-home-platform-new-certification-program/; Retrieved October 2014

by externals. However, the success of the platform depends on the number of integrated devices by third-party producers of domestic appliances and equipment. Consumers can purchase both singular modules as well as pre-commissioned kits representing an extendable solution.

Partitioning

In its most basic form, the SmartThings platform consists of a 'hub' which connects to all kinds of sensors in the home and a corresponding smart phone device allowing to control the platform. External Devices ("Things") represent a certain 'device type' which can be either generic (e.g. a thermostat) or it can be specific to a certain manufacturer or model, such as a Honewell thermostat. The second main component is the main platform app running on a smart phone, representing the 'brain' of the platform[37] .

Interfaces

SmartThings is modularized to foster the integration of third-party hardware modules and software solutions. The hub constitutes the central piece to which external third-party devices are connected. It supports standard interfaces like Ethernet, Zigbee or Z-Wave to allow connecting all kinds of external devices[38].

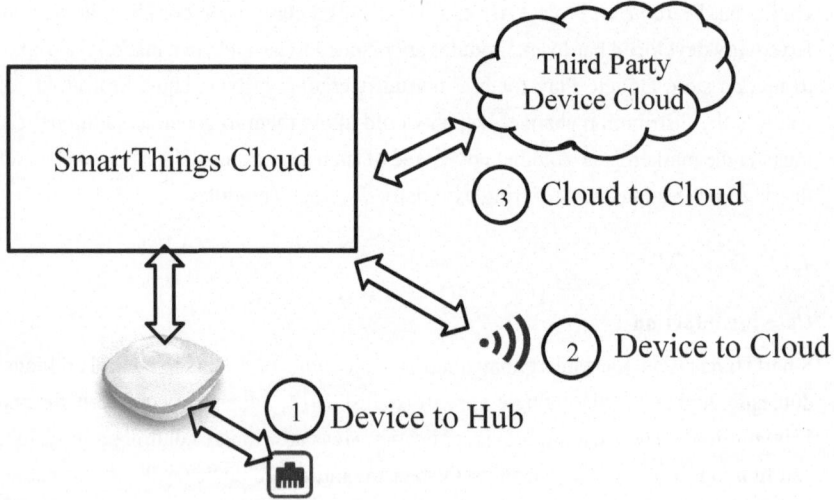

Figure 11 Smart Things cloud integration (according to SmartThings[39])

---

[37] See http://www.slashgear.com/smartthings-review-living-in-the-smart-home-17341453/; Retrieved October 2014
[38] See http://www.cnet.com/news/smart-home-showdown-wink-vs-smartthings/; Retrieved October 2014
[39] https://support.smartthings.com/hc/en-us/articles/200901290-Maker-Introduction; Retrieved October 2014

Overall, there are three different ways to integrate external devices, which are depicted in Figure 11:

- Device-to-Hub Integration: Devices are directly connected to the hub. This represents the standard way to integrate external devices.

- Device-to-Cloud Integration: For this type of integration, the hub is not needed, as the device is directly integrated to the SmartThings cloud via the Internet Protocol, e.g. by using Wi-Fi

- Cloud-to-Cloud Integration: This allows communicating with a third-party cloud, where external devices are not directly integrated but via the interfaces of the external cloud.

One particular example for the external cloud integration is the integration of the web-based automation platform 'If this than that' (IFTTT) [40], enabling the execution of cloud-based services in response to events triggered by the SmartThings platform. In addition, the SmartThings platform can also react to external events, which are not generated by the components of the SmartThings platform. Thus, it is also possible to communicate with devices not integrated with SmartThings but indirectly through the IFTTT platform. Such an external event could for instance originate from a weather forecasting cloud service, such as the forecasting of rain or certain temperatures.

Abstraction

To facilitate development, the distinct capabilities of a particular device are abstracted, so software applications ("SmartApps") can work with generic devices without having to develop for each specific device. Thus, developers work with a virtual representation of a device. This is ensured by 'device-type handlers' which act as a bridge between the generic capabilities of the virtual representation and the actual device respectively the protocol-specific interface[41]. Developers who want to integrate a specific device into the platform therefore need to write a specific device-type handler.

Encountered forms of openness

The viability of SmartThings is to a large degree dependent on the integration of external devices as the value increases with the number of appliances controlled by the platform. Developers can extend the SmartThings platform with both additional hardware as well as software modules. Additional software can be classified in three different types:

---

[40] See https://ifttt.com/smartthings; Retrieved October 2014
[41] http://docs.smartthings.com/en/latest/device-type-developers-guide/; Retrieved October 2014

Event-Handlers, Solution Modules and Service Managers[42]. The majority of community-developed apps are Event-Handlers, which react to an event triggered by external devices and executes custom code. Custom code could for instance execute commands on other devices, allowing to implement rules which control the smart home platform. Solution Modules are applications residing in the dashboard of the SmartThings mobile app, which act as containers for other SmartApps. Thus, the solution modules are a combination of existing software capabilities. At the time of writing, these solution modules are still built by the SmartThings team, however, it is planned to open them up for external development. The third category, service manager SmartApps act as the glue between device type handlers and the unique protocols of the integrated devices. Services provided by external devices are discovered and maintained by service managers. Whereas these three classes of apps refer to software directly run on the platform, it is also possible to integrate cloud-based services. The integration with IFTTT is an example for integrating cloud service. In terms of hardware openness, SmartThings is open for a broad variety of external devices, with the possibility to integrate devices with proprietary protocol standards by implementing corresponding device types. This implies, that there is basically no limit which kind of devices can be integrated.

Degree of openness

The degree of openness in this case follows a closed-core, open-periphery logic. SmartThings holds control over the main module, which integrates the peripheral parts supplied by externals. Thus, the core of the platform consists of the components, which integrate the platform as a whole. Although externals are themselves responsible for integrating additional hardware parts, the integration effort, which is demanded by externals, only refers to their additional modules, but they do not have the chance to change the core of the system.

4.2.6 LEGO Mindstorms

Case introduction

LEGO Mindstorms has already been discussed in the first study, however from a different perspective. Whereas the focus in the former study was to explore unintended open innovation (by hacking), the LEGO case in this study is explored from an openness perspective.

---

[42] See http://docs.smartthings.com/en/latest/introduction/; Retrieved October 2014

The term LEGO is nowadays almost proverbially used to describe modular structures due to its wide popularity and its memorable bricks, which are the basic building blocks for every LEGO design. Though LEGO products have been rather known as toy products for children, LEGO Mindstorms still offers an interesting case as it provides a modular platform with a great variety of computing elements allowing in particular the construction of programmable robotics. The platform was first introduced in 1998 and since September 2013, the third generation (LEGO Mindstorms EV 3) has been released. The platform is designed for young people without experience in robotics. Thus, it reflects a similar scenario as 'serious' platforms which try to allow open innovation for non-expert users.

Partitioning

LEGO Mindstorms includes to a broad variety of bricks in different forms and shapes the following ES components: 2 x Large Interactive Servo Motors, 1 x Medium Interactive Servo Motor, a color sensor, a touch sensor, an infrared sensor, an infrared beacon and the EV3 Intelligent Brick[43]. The EV3 Intelligent Brick is the core component of the electronical parts of LEGO Mindstorms and features an ARM9-based processor with Linux running on it[44].

Interfaces

The extensibility and flexibility of LEGO in general can be attributed to its modular brick concept, which allows to easily physically connect varying LEGO bricks. Thus, building complex designs is quite simple, but is not suited to professional use cases regarding its material properties. Regarding its embedded system part, LEGO Mindstorms offers LEGO Mindstorms offers standard interfaces such as an USB and an SD interface with which other Lego Mindstorms components can be connected. On the software side, Lego Mindstorms provides corresponding APIs, which allow users to develop their own applications.

Abstraction

LEGO Mindstorms especially targets young users for whom the platform is a mixture between education and entertainment. Although LEGO Mindstorms is designed to be a robotic platform aiming to give the user as much freedom as possible, the complexity of robotic development is to a large degree hidden. With its graphical development environment, LEGO Mindstorms hides the complexity of underlying programming, which

---

[43] see http://www.lego.com/de-de/mindstorms/support/faq/ Retrieved October 2014
[44] See http://makezine.com/2013/08/02/lego-mindstorms-ev3-source-code-available/; Retrieved October 2014

addresses foremost young users without a lot of expertise in programming respectively robotics. Therefore, users do not have to have in-depth knowledge about the algorithms usually needed to work with robotic actuators.

Encountered forms of openness

With its use of the Linux operating system, LEGO Mindstorms has embraced open source on the software level, inviting developers to make changes to the code base[45]. The source code has been uploaded by LEGO on the code sharing platform Github[46]. As a development kit, LEGO Mindstorms ships with a graphical programming environment, but can also be programmed with different programming languages, e.g. ROBOTC, which is based on the C programming language. The Mindstorms platform is also open for other programming languages, among others Java[47].

On the hardware layer, LEGO Mindstorms remains proprietary. LEGO Mindstorms' modularity allows the (re-) combination of existing modules in order to develop a custom solution. User can use existing, LEGO -provided modules, but LEGO does not provide a possibility for an integration of external hardware components. Due to it being programmable, it nonetheless offers a broad range of flexibility to develop custom solutions.

Degree of openness

As LEGO Mindstorms is not used for professional purposes, but has been mainly designed for children to experiment with robotic design, openness for additional hardware modules is not a necessary requirement. From a technical point of view, it would be possible that LEGO provides an open interface allowing third-party hardware components to be integrated. However, it is not certain whether this would be interesting from a commercial point of view for LEGO. By controlling the hardware layer, LEGO Mindstorms is also able to appropriate all earnings from the platform. Controlling the application layer is not strictly necessary from a business point of view, as LEGO does not receive any earnings by software applications on top of it. Rather, users should be stimulated to develop their own use cases on top of the Lego Mindstorms platform.

---

[45] See http://makezine.com/2013/08/02/lego-mindstorms-ev3-source-code-available/; Retrieved October 2014
[46] See https://github.com/mindboards/ev3sources; Retrieved October 2014
[47] See http://brickinthecloud.com/2013/11/14/programming-the-new-lego-mindstorms-ev3/; Retrieved October 2014

4.2.7 INCA

Case introduction

Although today's digital cameras have an increasing number of functions, they are usually designed for economies of scale leaving hardly any room to change their functionality after they have been released on the market. Especially industrial partners with the need for special image processing requirements usually need to work together with a camera manufacturer in order to implement their specific requirements. However, such cameras leave little room for flexibility. The Fraunhofer Society therefore decided to develop an open camera based on a different hardware and software architecture, which would allow a more flexible approach towards implementing customer-specific functions. Their model of an open camera allows the development of additional applications, similar to apps in the smart phone domain. As today's camera architectures usually do not allow the implementation of additional applications by the users, they had to come up with a novel camera architecture. The case at hand is largely based on interview data. Additional presentations supplied by Fraunhofer have also been incorporated in this case.

Architecture and partitioning

Traditionally, digital cameras are based on a FPGA (Field Programmable Gate Array) which is an integrated circuit programmed after manufacturing. After this initial programming an FPGA remains unchanged during its lifetime. This customization is usually very costly and requires a lot of development effort. After a FPGA has been configured for a special purpose, implementing new functions on it would still be possible but requires a thorough technical understanding regarding FPGA development. In addition, the FPGA does not provide a standardized developer interfaces. However, one of the advantages of using FPGAs is that it is usually cheaper when producing them on a lower scale. In contrast to the traditional design, which is built on a FPGA, the INCA is built on a SoC produced by Texas Instruments as its central component. A SoC has all the major components of a system put on a single chip which leads to less modularity regarding hardware components.

This change in the hardware architecture, in particular the use of a SoC also has a couple of implications on the overlying software layers. In general, it can be said, that the required know-how, effort and IP moves from the hardware to the software layers (interview).

The lowest software layer part of the SoC is the Ducati framework, which delivers low-level drivers for access to the hardware. This layer is also referred to as the hardware abstraction layer. It cannot be changed by users, as it is closed source. The most crucial change which illustrates the move from hardware to software is the use of Android as an operating system which allows a wide range of applications to be built on top of it and abstracts the underlying technical complexity. Therefore, the interview partner also compared the architecture of the INCA camera with common smart phone architectures.

Interfaces

The Android operating system offers application developers APIs for accessing the hardware without knowing details about the underlying technical implementation. Regarding the extensibility for additional hardware devices, the SoC comes with a certain set of interfaces which cannot be changed during run-time but would need to be indirectly attached, e.g. by a more general interface (interview).

Abstraction

Facilitating software applications through abstraction of lower layers is a rather common design principle. The modular design principle of abstraction is often used to hide the complexity of underlying layers to upper layers. In the case of INCA, this design principle is used for the Ducati framework, which hides the hardware details to upper layers. The layer on top of Ducati (the Android operating system) also further abstracts hardware-specific details.

Encountered forms of openness

Due to its architecture built on a SoC, all computing parts are integrated on a single chip. Replacing hardware modules therefore would require a complete replacement of the SoC. This means, that the additional flexibility for new software functions gained by a SoC constrains the flexibility regarding hardware. However, the SoC comes with a variety of standardized interfaces, e.g. USB. By using an adapter, USB can also be used for different interface standards, e.g. Ethernet, serial interface or an analog audio interface.

The openness for new software in turn is also constrained by the underlying hardware and by the functions the middleware provides to the upper software layers. Fraunhofer would be able to make changes on these layers, but it would be closed for customers. New software applications for the INCA are based on the APIs exposed by the Android operating system. In most cases, this can be done independently without changing underlying layers. Using an open operating system like Android facilitates the integration of software modules, because it already offers an "App"-concept that acts as a frame for modularization of new software functions. Furthermore, Android also offers a Software

Development Kit (SDK), which facilitates the development and testing of new applications. In some cases, enhancing the software functionality requires changes on deeper layers. For instance, customizations regarding the compression or how exactly the sensor data is handed over to the Android OS is part of the Ducati framework. In order to change the behavior of this layer, the interface on the Android side needs to be customized too. This implies that customizing the camera for different use cases may need additional integration procedures.

Degree of openness

The chosen degree of openness leaves the control of the underlying hardware platform to Fraunhofer. This implies that changes to the hardware base for specific customer requirements has to be done in cooperation with Fraunhofer. This openness strategy allows Fraunhofer to appropriate returns when the camera is used for new use cases which require changes on lower layers or of the hardware base. This includes for instance the integration of a different camera sensor.

4.2.8 Prosyst E-Health

Case introduction

E-Health is an emerging domain drawing on medical informatics, public health and business which relates to health services and information provided by the internet and other technologies (Eysenbach 2001). This case deals with the e-health platform mBS which allows integrating various embedded technologies which deliver e-health services. The platform is delivered by Prosyst, a German software company focusing on offering middleware for the Internet of Things. In the eHealth domain, they offer OSGi-based (Open Service Gateway Initiative) middleware enabling their customers to build flexible and modular e-health platforms. The mBS platform can be used by customers to build their own e-health solution. Customers can enhance the platform by developing specific e-health services but also open their platforms for complementary applications.

The case at hand is largely based on interview data.

Architecture and partitioning

The Prosyst mBS platform is an OSGi based modular platform which provides mechanisms to easily change and add both hardware and software modules. OSGi as a framework for realizing modular software solutions is already widely established in different application domains. Prosyst itself does not sell an e-health platform to end customers but enables firms (mostly telecommunication firms) to choose their own hardware platform, on which they implement Prosyst mBS and develop services for this platform. Establishing an open platform in the eHealth domain, however, holds additional challenges.

Interfaces and abstraction

How the software components interact with each other is already widely determined by the OSGi framework, which standardizes components and corresponding interfaces.

On the hardware layer, the interoperability of devices from different manufacturers is achieved by following the interoperability guidelines specified by the Continua Alliance, a standards selection body consisting of a variety of industry actors. The goal of Continua is to establish interoperable connected health solutions, which enable personalized health and wellness management[48]. By providing a set of supported standards, device manufacturers can ensure the interoperability of their devices. Being standards-conform decreases switching costs between different sensors, as long as these conform to the same standards (Wartena, Muskens, and Schmitt 2009).

Another field requiring interoperability concerns the exchange of vital signs data between different devices. The ISO/IEEE 11073[49] group of norms describes the components of a system required for data exchange and evaluation of this class of data.

Encountered forms of openness

Technically, building on the Prosyst eHealth platform allows both for openness on the application software layer as well as on the hardware layer. For hardware manufacturers, providing e.g. additional sensors requires that they are compatible to the standards, which have been laid out by the Continua Alliance. In contrast to a closed approach, switching costs between different sensors would be much lower (Wartena, Muskens, and Schmitt 2009), therefore leading to more hardware openness.

On the software layer, the platform is open for additional software applications. However, platform providers using Prosyst mBS often charge externals for becoming a certified partner, and in addition, new applications need to be licensed by the platform provider. Moreover, legal requirements add an additional layer of complexity for application developers. Therefore, new software applications for the platform would usually be provided by a small ecosystem of specialized suppliers in the healthcare field.

---

[48] See http://www.continuaalliance.org/about-the-alliance retrieved August 2013
[49] See https://standards.ieee.org/findstds/standard/healthcare_it.html retrieved August 2013

Realizing openness for medical applications has certain additional requirements, as software for medical purposes is subject to legal requirements that specify the installation, operation and maintenance of medical products. If the software particularly serves diagnostic or therapeutic goals, it would be categorized as a medical product (Gärtner 2010). Depending on potential threats, devices are classified in different categories which require different procedures towards conformity evaluation, documentation and quality ensurance procedures. In terms of openness, this implies, that external contributors must meet certain requirements concerning certification of their developed applications. This constrains potential contributors as it requires explicit domain knowledge. According to the interview partner, the partners of e-health platforms are often specialized organizations or enterprises that are already established in the healthcare industry.

Regarding hardware openness, the great variety of different devices and communication standards requires the platform to be widely compatible to different standards. So, one of the main tasks of Prosyst was to enhance OSGi to fit in this context. However, not only the platform itself, but also the different hardware vendors must fit to these standards. The standards these companies need to implement in order to be compatible have been laid out by the Continua Alliance, a standards selection body founded by a variety of industry actors.

Degree of openness

E-Health platforms like Prosyst mBS are to a wide degree dependent on the contribution by externals, both for the development of additional software applications as well as for the integration of third-party devices. At the same time, openness needs to be constrained to such a degree that legal requirements, such as the need for certification is ensured. Therefore, adopters of such an e-health platform would most likely allow externals to develop additional applications but would rather control the core parts of the platform in order to appropriate returns and to protect IP.

4.2.9 Infotainment System

Case introduction

Infotainment systems take a special position in the overall IT architecture of cars. First of all, they are less safety-critical, as they usually do not provide vital functions controlling the driving behavior of the car. Nonetheless, their importance is growing, as consumer demands with regard to additional services like navigation, traffic jam avoidance, information and entertainment are increasing. At the same time, customers are used to fast innovation cycles in other contexts, e.g. consumer electronics and expect new functions also in the after-market as well as the seamless integration of car's infotainment system with other consumer devices like smart phone or tablet PCs. By request of our contact, this case has been anonymized. This case is based on interview data and material presented by the company at hand.

Architecture and partitioning

The infotainment system is one of a variety of systems, which controls the electronic functionalities of a car. It is separated from the other systems in order to ensure a certain level of isolation to increase safety and security. This isolation also allows to individually analyze the modularity of the infotainment (sub-)system without showing the interdependencies with other systems. For instance, the components of the infotainment system communicate on a separate bus system.

Regarding the hardware, parts of the infotainment system are based on consumer technology and not on specifically manufactured hardware as it is often found in embedded systems. However, there is the requirement of certification for automotive use. With such a hardware platform, the infotainment provider wants to enable similar capabilities as in consumer hardware, for instance software reusability or hardware upgrades. The hardware platform for the infotainment function is based on around eight different CPUs. This is due to the diverging requirements of the different infotainment functions. Such a partitioning also allows separating traditional infotainment functions with higher dependability requirements from additional functions with less critical requirements. Some of these traditional applications are for instance subject to real-time constraints, which can thus be ensured on parts or the system. This reflects the need to achieve similar innovation cycle times for parts of the system as found in consumer products.

On the software side, the architecture is also designed to allow integrating additional functions to the system. As a base for the overall architecture, the infotainment system makes use of the OSGi Framework, which facilitates the installation and change of software components. The OSGi framework is a component architecture resting on Java used across different industries to facilitate the modular integration of various components.

Interfaces

A feature not yet implemented but currently in the planning stage is the provision of certain functions via a wireless connection, thus giving access to parts of the infotainments systems' functions via a centralized interface. This will allow to steer certain functions through external devices, such as via smart phone or via tablet.

Abstraction

The case data did not reveal further insights regarding this category of modular design rules. This does not imply that this modular design rule is not applied in the design of the system, but that no specific requirements for abstraction regarding openness have been found.

Encountered forms of openness

From a practical perspective, switching particular hardware modules is only possible to a limited degree as the plug contacts are partly constructed only for a limited number of switching. At the same time, the hardware is subject to tight cost saving aspects. Therefore, it relies on proprietary, optimized components, which also involves finding the best configuration in terms of performance. This, in turn, increases the coupling between different components, thus leading to a more integral configuration of the hardware components. In terms of openness, this can be a disadvantage, as these specific components often are less standardized and have more independencies among each other.

On the software level, the following forms of openness were found:

Although there is a software development kit for partners, due to high quality requirements, the OEM has to explicitly allow new software. Becoming a partner also involves several steps like contract relationships with the OEM and the fulfillment of particular standards in terms of the development process. Furthermore, openness for new applications also has to consider real-time requirements, which need to be considered when providing new functions.

For this reason, openness in terms of deploying new software modules on the existing platform is limited to special use cases that will be described in the next paragraphs.

One use case for openness is to integrate third-party devices like smart phone or tablets. The OEM offers a software module, which enables a smart phone app to stream media content, e.g. music to the infotainment system, in order to use the car sound system.

An additional way to opening their system currently in the development is to offer certain interfaces via a wireless connection. Potential use cases would be for instance to remotely manage certain functions, e.g. to control air conditioning. Although this does not offer completely new functions, it allows extending existing applications to different devices. Thus, new functions do not necessarily have to be executed on the same system. Rather, the infotainment system can also be seen as a front-end for applications executed on an online backend. Examples for such additional services would be the possibility to display weather services or prices of gas stations. Another option would be to create a mash-up based on local data, e.g. GPS data of the vehicle in combination with additional map layers to create an integrated map application.

Degree of openness

The degree of openness in the infotainment case is mostly restrained by safety and real-time considerations. The analysis of the Infotainment's modularity has already shown that the system is partitioned in alignment with safety requirements. Although external apps running e.g. on smart phones or tablets can access certain system's functions, the infotainment firm keeps control which applications are installed directly on their own system.

4.2.10 John Deere

Case introduction

John Deere is one of the largest firms in the field of agricultural equipment technology. They offer a wide variety of different agricultural machinery like tractors, harvesters, seeders etc. In general, the agricultural sector is becoming more and more digitalized with agricultural machinery being equipped with additional hardware and software components. These additional components deliver functions like more effective fertilization, improved fleet management or more efficiency in terms of fuel consumption. The case for openness for John Deere machinery is especially driven by the need to allow coupling of the tractors with trailers from different manufacturers. Some trailers are only produced by manufacturers specialized in a particular niche market, which John Deere itself does not serve. By allowing these manufacturers to couple their trailers with machinery from John Deere, it is able to serve these markets. The case at hand is largely based on interview data and on additional material.

Architecture and partitioning

The architecture of John Deere tractors is similar to other vehicle architectures, insofar that it is based on different electronic control units, which are connected via a central bus system, the Controller Area Network bus (CAN bus). The CAN bus cannot be directly accessed by externals, but through the terminal provided by John Deere. This terminal therefore acts like a proxy, as direct access to the CAN bus would violate safety constraints. Using this approach, John Deere can still exercise control over their vehicle platform. Via the gateway, various high-level functions like the documentation of carried out work (e.g. planting or fertilizer output) or the integration of mobile devices are carried out. To further increase safety, the control of certain critical systems like steering, speed control etc. is running on their own controlling units.

Interfaces

As externals cannot directly access the CAN bus, John Deere vehicles offer a second bus system, the ISOBUS, which constitutes a standard communication protocol for agricultural machinery (ISO 11783)[50]. The ISOBUS enables externals to transmit their process data in order to be used by additional software applications. Moreover, John Deere also provides access to certain functions and data via the ISOBUS. The need for the ISOBUS resulted mainly due to the different requirements in the agricultural sector often demanding specialized hardware machinery which John Deere cannot deliver. The need for specialized solutions is also driven by legal requirements in different countries However, the CAN bus cannot be directly accessed for these use cases, as allowing access to it would endanger existing functions, e.g. due to time criticality of critical functions. To allow for a seamless integration, the producers of these external machineries must be able to access certain interfaces of the tractor. Partners cooperating more closely with John Deere can get more access to certain interfaces respectively APIs.

Abstraction

As it has been shown, externals do not have direct access to the CAN bus. However, the terminal takes the role of an abstraction layer giving limited access to some functions which are accessed through the CAN bus. Additional applications supplied by externals can thus gain access to certain functions via the terminal.

Encountered forms of openness

There are several scenarios for openness of John Deere's agricultural vehicles. The main case is to allow other machinery producers to integrate their trailers with the tractors from John Deere. This includes not only attaching the devices to the tractors, but also to integrate the embedded systems in these different devices. The second use case is based on data access. Due to legal requirements, farmers have to record data to document certain agricultural process. Furthermore, the data can be also used to optimize certain processes like crop planting or fertilizing.

---

[50] For details, see http://www.iso.org/iso/iso_catalogue/catalogue_tc/catalogue_detail.htm?csnumber=54390; Retrieved October 2013

For third parties, the gateway mainly provides a possibility to access process data (i.e. the data generated through the work processes), but most vehicle data can only be accessed by software applications provided by John Deere. This data can for instance be accessed via mobile devices, but John Deere also offers integration in the cloud. In addition, the vehicles are also dirigible, for instance to calculate optimal lanes in order to save fuel. Thus, the gateway does not only allow data access, but also to access diverse vehicle functions. It also provides the user interface allowing to control different applications. The user interface itself is extendable for third party applications, which for instance allows to steer the corresponding trailer. Due to safety reasons, integrating new solutions on the vehicle platform by John Deere requires certification, which raises additional challenges to developers.

Degree of openness

By providing open interfaces for additional machinery, John Deere is exposed to the risk of imitation by other firms. Therefore, they need to provide additional value to the customer, which would motivate them to use the trailers. The partitioning of the vehicle interfaces in two separate bus systems, the CAN bus and the ISOBUS can therefore be seen not only as a safety measure, but also as a way to protect certain parts of the system from competitors. As John Deere produces its own trailers, it can benefit from the direct access to the CAN bus, which allows them to design their products in a more integrated fashion and therefore with more attuned functions. On the other hand, competitors can still access the ISOBUS giving them access to the most important functions. It also offers John Deere the possibility to strategically decide, what vehicle functions and data should be accessible via the ISOBUS.

The gateway implemented by John Deere also supports protecting core assets. It can be used as a graphical user interface for external partners where John Deere provides specific interfaces and "placeholders" for add-ons by externals.

4.2.11 Kuka Youbot

Case introduction

The current case deals with the robotics platform Youbot developed by Kuka. The platform itself is not aimed at commercialization, but serves as a platform for research and education. According to the product manager of Youbot, this platform can be seen as a scaled down version of the products they offer, but with the potential to pursue research in a variety of fields ranging from exploring new sensor concepts on a hardware layer, to exploring new applications based on the Youbot platform. In terms of open innovation, they also use the platform for innovation awards for innovative ideas built on the Youbot. Openness is an important characteristic of the Youbot platform in order to maximize research opportunities and enable education based on the Youbot robotics platform.

Architecture and partitioning

The Youbot itself does not prescribe specific use cases. Rather, it is designed for experimenting and to stimulate learning. Therefore, it does not prescribe a particular operating system or software but leaves this open to the community. The community supplies the so-called Youbot-driver, which provides hardware access and thus functions as an operating system. In addition, the community also provides plug-ins allowing to control certain hardware parts of the Youbot.

Interfaces

Due to its broad application areas, interface standardization plays a big role. To install additional hardware modules, the Youbot is equipped with the most common hardware interfaces like USB, Ethercat etc. In addition, the Youbot is designed in such a way, that additional hardware components can be easily attached to the Youbot. Attaching additional hardware modules to a particular spot is not always straightforward, but is also subject to research. Therefore, for the Youbot, not only the existence of interfaces to exchange information plays a role, but also interfaces which facilitate the placement of additional HW components.

Abstraction

Due to its educational purpose, one aim of the Youbot is to give the users the chance to experiment with the specifics of the hardware and in particular with the specifics of robotic development. Thus, Kuka itself does not provide additional abstraction layers hiding the complexity of the underlying hardware. However, users can make use of community-developed software plug-ins for the Youbot so they do not necessarily need to engage with the hardware specifics.

Encountered forms of openness

The Youbot offers a high degree of software openness as well as hardware openness. On the software layer, Kuka does not dictate any specific operating system or software that should be run on the Youbot. Rather, users of the platform can basically use the Youbot with every available software. In terms of hardware, it is encouraged to build on the existing hardware base by connecting all kinds of sensors, actuators and other additional modules. Exploring how additional hardware like sensors can interact with the Youbot platform is one of the particular research goals addressed by Kuka.

In terms of its SW architecture, the Youbot is quite open, as Kuka does not deliver it with pre-installed SW. However, the standard configuration implies installing Youbot driver, which is a community-based software allowing to control the robot.

Degree of openness

In this particular case, the decision what parts of the system should be opened and which parts should remain closed is not so much influenced by matters of value appropriation, but more by the implications of openness on conducting research and enabling education. The trade-off between openness and closeness is rather determined by the notion of offering an easy-to-use platform but at the same time, to leave room for innovation to a high degree. Due to its non-commercial orientation and its focus on education and research, Kuka does not centralize additional developments for the Youbot, but rather relies on the community itself to exchange experiences and improve the software and hardware base. Therefore, they also do not provide standardized integration processes of additional modules. As they do not commercialize user innovations based on the Youbot, they also do not have to take responsibility in terms of its proper functioning.

4.2.12 Qivicon

Case introduction

Qivicon is a smart home platform by the German telecommunication company Deutsche Telekom which allows the integration of a broad variety of devices ranging from heating systems, power supply to all kinds of sensors and actuators. It provides extensibility options for partners and developers to enable them to develop new software applications as well as to allow integrating new devices. The central building block of the platform is the Qivicon Home Base, a small computer, which controls the integrated devices. New software applications by partners also run on the Home Base. In addition, the home base can also be accessed by external devices, e.g. to allow cloud integration.

Architecture

The realization of these forms of openness has certain architectural requirements that the Qivicon platform needed to take into account. In general, the gateway is a Linux-based system on which the Java Embedded Edition runs. On top of it, the OSGi platform, which provides a high level of software modularity, also facilitates adding new hardware devices to the platform. To account for the requirements of different software applications, additional services like scheduling mechanisms, job management etc. are needed.

To ensure security and stability of the gateway, new software applications are deployed in a sandbox environment, which provides constrained access to the system's resources. A sandbox can for instance be used to allow a software application to control an external device, but does not allow accessing certain system resources like local files. A second type of sandbox is provided for software applications, which include a driver for a device which has not yet been integrated. This kind of sandbox needs enhanced permissions on the system level.

Interfaces

The attractiveness of the Qivicon platforms for customers grows with the amount of different devices and standards the platform supports. For this sake, the Qivicon development team tries to integrate the most common connection standards, to easily integrate new devices. For more exotic connection standards, they still leave room for external partners to integrate their own standards.

To allow for cloud integration, interfaces respectively APIs are not only offered for software running on the gateway itself, but also to provide web services to allow for connections via the web. This also permits external devices like tablet PCs or smart phones to access the functions of the gateway.

Abstraction

Based on the OSGi platform, additional APIs have been developed to provide the 'device abstraction', which allows hardware-independent access of different devices and can be understood as an abstraction layer. The goal of the device abstraction is to interact with the corresponding devices independently from its underlying protocol.

Encountered forms of openness

On the Qivicon platform, several kinds of openness can be identified. First of all, it allows the user to develop additional software applications. These applications can for instance control different devices integrated in the platform. For instance, one category of software applications which have been developed by partners are general-purpose applications not specific to a particular device but allowing the management of different devices. The second type of openness takes place at the hardware level. New devices can be integrated on the platform by device manufacturers requiring them to develop additional drivers. The third type of openness is based on cloud integration. The home base and its services can be accessed via the cloud through corresponding interfaces provided by the home base. Besides the modular design rules Qivicon implements to foster external development, they also offer a SDK targeting external partners and developers. To ensure the quality of applications developed by externals, Qivicon also needs to ensure, that new applications running on the gateway do not violate software licenses and, in addition, do not violate data security.

Degree of openness

Regarding the degree of openness, the Qivicon platform follows a rather open approach. It does not restrain customers to use the Qivicon-based software platform to control external devices, but relies on its partners to come up with corresponding software solutions. This openness allows device manufacturers or other developers to differentiate themselves with additional functions rather than being constrained by an already existing software platform. Qivicon itself controls the core hardware components, namely the Qivicon home base, and the operating system layer, thus keeping control of the further evolvement of the platform.

4.2.13 RACE

Case introduction

RACE (Robust and reliable Automotive Computing Environment for future eCars) is a research project started in 2012 by eight partners from industry and research in order to develop a new architecture for electrical vehicles. RACE is coordinated by Siemens, a big German engineering firm. The current modularization of the architecture corresponds to the mechanical structure of the car. The new architecture will be based on a centralized control platform, a homogeneous communication backbone and the concept of smart sensors/actuators. New software, such as driver assistance, security and infotainment functions, can hence be provided as software packages without installation of new control devices. Moreover, the architecture supports plug-and-play (PnP), i.e. the possibility to deploy new software and hardware functions for existing cars in the aftermarket. This way, the need to add new hardware to realize new functions is minimized and instead new functions are installed purely as software modules[51].

Architecture

The requirements for an architecture, which supports 'plug-and-play' of new hardware and software lies at the core of the RACE project. The envisaged architecture will be

---

[51] see http://www.projekt-race.de/upload/downloads/PI_Race_2013-02-20.pdf; Retrieved October 2013

highly centralized in contrast to current IT architectures in cars, which makes use of up to 90 electronic control units (ECUs). Often, new functions are developed as a combination of separate hardware and software modules including sensors and actuators instead of centralizing different software functions on a common hardware platform (Fortiss 2011). As these ECUs are highly specific, there is also much less flexibility to implement new functions, as they are designed for a specific purpose and are often highly dependent on one another. By reducing the number of required ECUs and restructuring the SW architecture, the system complexity (e.g. number of dependencies) will be highly reduced. Implementing a central system requires additional mechanism for coordination, for instance, the central system uses PikeOS as an operating system, which provides resource management, so a particular function cannot claim too many resources (interview).

According to Fortiss (2011), not only the central system is redesigned, but the role of peripheral devices like sensors is subject to change as well. Enhancing the sensors with additional intelligence allows them to be integrated in a communication network. Without platform-neutral development and distribution of software, this would hardly be possible (Fortiss 2011).

As this architecture is quite ambitious when comparing it with today's IT architecture in cars, RACE came up with two approaches towards implementation of the proposed architecture: a revolutionary approach and an evolutionary approach. Whereas by following the revolutionary approach, the whole legacy architecture would be replaced by the new one, whereas by following the evolutionary approach, OEMs would implement the new architecture for a particular domain of their IT architecture and would integrate additional parts of the system in the new architecture step-by-step.

Interfaces

To facilitate access to sensors, RACE provides a common interface, which allows developers to access sensor data without having to care about the technical implementation and the details of communication to the sensor (interview). This separation of hardware and software in order to work with a hardware-independent interface is provided by an additional layer, the middleware. This is an example where abstraction helps to hide complexity and develop modules independently. Another advantage of this approach is that it allows hardware-independent development of new software. Next to standardized interfaces to the hardware, the interface to the application layer needs to provide plug-and-play mechanisms which allows the integration of new components and functions (Fortiss 2011).

By abstracting the technical details of the actual implementation, the development of new functions is facilitated. Furthermore, by using standardized interfaces to peripheral hardware like sensors, also the replacement of sensors would be facilitated. In contrast to today's sensors, they would be more 'intelligent', allowing to use them for different purposes.

Abstraction

One goal of the RACE project is to abstract the complexity in certain modules and to give access to systems functions via standardized interfaces. However, developers still need certain domain knowledge, however less than before, as they can develop based on standardized APIs. Thus, developers must possess general knowledge regarding embedded systems development. Functional knowledge is still required, but not at the same level of detail, but rather on an architectural level.

Encountered forms of openness

The proposed architecture allows openness on both the hardware level as well as on the application level. As a car is a safety-critical system, there are certain constraints when implementing new SW functions or replacing HW. First of all, adequate testing procedures must be in place when changing particular components of a system, with stricter constraints for parts which are more safety-critical.

On the hardware layer, the new architecture allows replacing or adding new sensors, actors or even the HW of the central computing platform. On a SW layer, the new architecture allows the ex-post implementation of new functions in order to provide additional services, however, the core functions (operating system, resource management etc.) remain closed.

Although the dependencies between different components are largely reduced, there is still a need for central control of the overall system due to safety and liability reasons. Allowing installing new application also poses a security risk, therefore appropriate mechanisms (e.g. digital signatures) are needed to ensure that the application has been developed by a trusted vendor (interview). Furthermore, the development process needs to take standardization and certification procedures into account. In particular, when developing safety-critical applications for the automotive domain, the ISO 26262 needs to be followed. However, by relying on the envisaged architecture, it would be enough to certify the singular component, and not the system as a whole (interview). A particular responsibility of the OEM in this distributed setting is quality insurance and to provide testing specifications (interview). Therefore, such an architecture enables a higher number of actors to be involved in the development of a car, but it still has to be centrally coordinated by the OEM, however, more due to organizational reasons than technical reasons.

Due to the complexity of the ES architecture in cars and due to the technical as well as organization requirements automotive producers encounter, RACE suggests two different ways toward openness. Both of these approaches are planned to be implemented in two electrical car prototypes:

- Revolutionary Approach: The prototype will completely be based on the new architecture developed by the RACE consortium
- Evolutionary Approach: this approach will incrementally replace the 'old' components with the 'new' components

Degree of openness

As the RACE project constitutes a research project, it is difficult to draw conclusions about risks and chances of a particular degree of openness. As the RACE architecture has not yet been implemented in an existing vehicle architecture, it is difficult to answer, which degree of openness should be pursued from both a technical as well as a business point of view. In general, openness for vehicle infotainment systems must conform to high safety and RT standards. Although the RACE architecture tackles these challenges, opening the vehicle ES architecture is associated with considerable risks. Furthermore, from an organizational point of view, opening the vehicle architecture would also lead to changes in the organization. Currently, automobile manufacturers are specifying the requirements for the ES components, and thus are also centrally planning the features of a particular vehicle. Automobile producers therefore must balance the need for central planning with the pursued degree of openness. The evolutionary approach towards openness outlined by RACE can support automobile producers implementing a particular degree of openness.

4.2.14 Commercial Vehicle Platform

Case introduction

This case is about the opening of ES in the context of construction machinery vehicles. Due to reasons of confidentiality, the case has been anonymized and focuses only on specific aspects in the context of our research question. The primary source of the case was an engineering company, which was responsible in providing an additional hardware module which allows access to the internal bus system of the construction machinery vehicles. Thus, the engineering company was both involved in planning as well as in the implementation of the opening of the construction machinery vehicle platform.

The data collected via the extra unit can be evaluated on a central platform which holds several benefits. First of all, it enables remote maintenance for service technicians which is particularly valuable when the machinery is deployed in remote locations. Secondly, construction enterprises can manage their fleets more effectively by having a detailed picture about the state of their machinery. Furthermore, there are additional features like for instance theft protection. By offering a web interface, customers can efficiently manage their fleet of construction machinery and have access to all kinds of vehicle data which provides the foundation for additional software applications.

However, although the vehicle platform is technically opened, the data is used by the vehicle provider itself for its own fleet management platform, but not for externals. Thus, this case can be used to compare it with other cases where a similar level of openness for externals is provided.

Architecture

The existing architecture of the construction machine itself is not subject to changes, as the additional data collection unit only needs read access to the data bus, but does not need any write access. New software applications are based on the vehicle data provided by an additional module in the vehicle architecture that has access to the central bus system (in the following Data-Access-Module (DAM)). As an execution context, these applications do not run on the vehicle or the DAM itself, but outside the vehicle's context on a separate platform. On the one hand, this offers additional flexibility, as new software applications would not be hardware-constrained. Furthermore, the further processing of the data does not have to take into account any other constraints by the internal system inside the construction equipment, but can be executed independently on an external platform. On the other hand, new software applications are solely based on processing existing data, but do not allow accessing other parts of the construction machine.

Therefore, the existing vehicle infrastructure is mostly left untouched. The data collection unit is designed in such a way, that it allows future enhancements in terms of its software.

Abstraction

The DAM itself not only constitutes an interface but also acts as an abstraction layer where the complexity of the underlying data and its specification is hidden. Thus, this approach could also be used to give access only to non-confidential data. This facilitates building additional data-based applications. In contrast to the three classical layers, this platform features an explicit 'data abstraction layer'.

Interfaces

To collect data from the construction machine, the central bus system provides the main interface for data collection. The bus system normally cannot be accessed by external parties but is accessed by the DAM as a proxy instead. Customers can access data via a web platform which allows creating new views based on the data provided by the DAM.

Encountered forms of openness

As it has been described in the part about the architecture of this case's ES, openness in this case is constrained to data-based software applications. This approach does not provide any possibility for software applications changing the functionality of the underlying vehicle itself. The goal of this degree of openness is to create additional services, which help to manage the vehicle, e.g. maintenance or a group of vehicles, e.g. fleet management. The hardware module which allows access to the system data may be changed by the provider in the future in order to provide additional data to externals.

The use cases for openness do not entail enhancing the hardware capabilities by customers, but is based on the existing hardware capabilities. The platform also does not provide any possibilities to change existing hardware.

Degree of openness

As it has been described, openness in this case is constrained to building data-based applications running externally of the ES. As the vehicle data can only be used by the vehicle providers own software platform, openness in this case does not lead to open innovation. For the vehicle producer, the use cases for additional software applications are still manageable. By opening the data also for externals, the producer would lose the ability to appropriate the returns of these additional services himself.

4.2.15 OpenXC

Case introduction

OpenXC is a joint project conducted by Ford in cooperation with Buglabs and Cross-Chasm with the goal of offering an API for the vehicle's data (Openxcplatform.com). Access to the vehicle's data is provided by installing an additional hardware module which is able to read and translate internal vehicle data. Built on this data, external developers can extend the vehicle by developing new applications and adding pluggable modules.

Architecture and partitioning

Although the goal of OpenXC is to extend a vehicle with new applications, the architecture of a car remains untouched. Instead, OpenXC allows to access the vehicle data by utilizing the ODB-II port to access the CAN bus. This is achieved by the "vehicle interface", a device that can read and translate CAN messages into a standard format. The second hardware component needed is a host device, e.g. an Android tablet, or a Python environment. However, OpenXC does not prescribe, on which host device new applications have to be run. The basic requirement for the host device is that it understands OpenXC vehicle data either via USB, Bluetooth or a network interface[52].

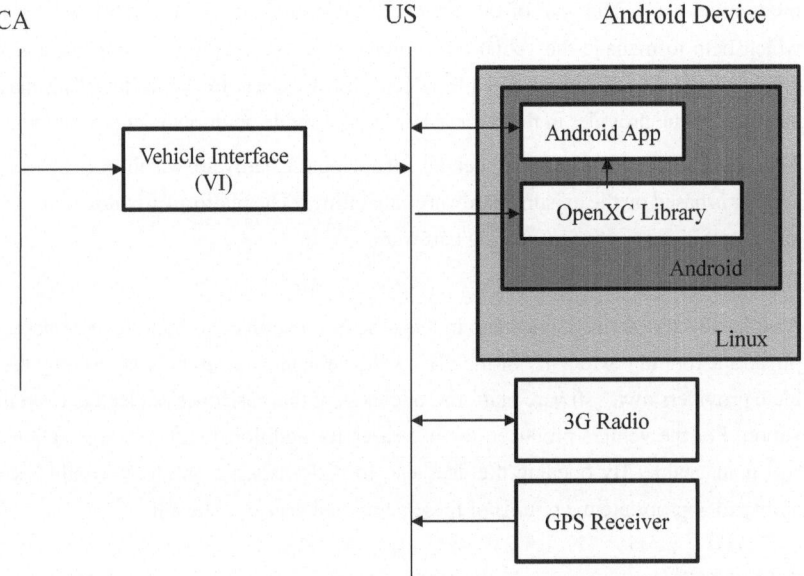

Figure 12 OpenXC architecture (according to http://openxcplatform.com/)

To minimize the footprint of this kind of data openness, additional applications run on an external device instead of being executed on the vehicle's system resources itself. This

---

[52] See http://openxcplatform.com/host-devices/hardware.html; Retrieved October 2013

architectural choice also help to keep costs low. The OpenXC vehicle interface can be purchased for $40[53].

Figure 12 depicts the basic architecture of the OpenXC platform.

Interfaces

As it can be seen in Figure 12, the OpenXC platform provides read-only access to the main bus system via a 'proxy module', the vehicle interface. The vehicle interface in turn provides access via USB, which represents a standardized interface. In addition, the vehicle data can also be accessed via Bluetooth or Ethernet/Wi-Fi. The vehicle interface provides only read-only access and does not allow write or execute operations.

Comparing the architecture of OpenXC with the construction vehicle case described before, it can be seen, that the approach towards openness is rather similar. Both cases feature an additional hardware module, which acts as an interface towards the vehicle data. In comparison to the construction vehicle case, openness in the OpenXC is performed to enable open innovation. This implies that openness for open innovation in this case does not necessarily differ from 'internal' openness when it comes to data access. The additional requirement for OpenXC is rather to give access only to a subset of data, which does not allow reverse engineering.

Abstraction

Additional applications are based on the vehicle data via the vehicle interface. Besides granting access to a subset of vehicle data, the vehicle interface acts as a CAN translator, that converts CAN messages into readable information (OpenXC message format) for external developers. Thus, the vehicle interface also acts as an additional abstraction layer through which external developers indirectly access the vehicle data[54].

Encountered forms of openness

Openness in the OpenXC case is rather limited as it is confined to granting read-access to the vehicle's data via the vehicle interface. Currently, there are no plans for further openness besides data access, as this would result in a broad range of security and liability risk[55]. The extent of access to the vehicle data can be determined by the vehicle producer, who can choose to release their CAN message definitions or providing a precompiled OpenXC translator binary.

---

[53] See http://openxcplatform.com/overview/index.html Retrieved October 2013
[54] See http://openxcplatform.com/overview/faq.html; Retrieved October 2013
[55] see http://techcrunch.com/2013/01/08/ford-launches-its-openxc-sdk-and-hardware-specs-to-let-developers-access-its-cars-sensors-and-metrics/; Retrieved February 2014

Additional applications need to be run on Android by using the OpenXC library. Developers can choose between OpenXC supports both developing Android as well as Python apps.

Degree of openness

Similarly to the construction vehicle case described before, OpenXC provides access to a subset of the vehicle data. Whereas in the construction vehicle case the ES was opened technically but not for externals, OpenXC specifically aims to allow external users to build software applications. One difference to the construction vehicle case can be seen in the type of services enabled by openness: for the construction vehicle case, there were clear use cases, which provide a base for differentiating from the competition and for generating additional earnings. Although OpenXC also aims to enable additional services, which benefit the user, they are less strategically important for an automotive company utilizing the OpenXC platform.

4.2.16 AutoPNP

Case introduction

AutoPNP (Auto Plug and Play) is a research project conducted by the Fraunhofer Society in cooperation with different industry partners with the goal of developing a software architecture for automation systems. The aim of the software architecture is to allow "plug and play" integration of hardware and software integration from different machine providers[56]. With the move from mass production to more individualized production processes, this flexibility in integrating different machines in the production process becomes increasingly important. The base of the developed software architecture is the middleware CHROMOSOME, which allows modelling production processes with the integrated machines.

Architecture and partitioning

In CHROMOSOME, functionalities are wrapped inside components that are accessible via "ports" which constitute standardized interfaces. The middleware itself runs on a central component, which integrates the different machines. If a certain devices cannot be directly connected to the middleware, e.g. when it is not compatible, an additional gateway has to be implemented to integrate the corresponding machine (documentation, interview).

---

[56] http://www.autopnp.com/; Retrieved February 2014

Interfaces

One crucial design aspect of CHROMOSOME is the standardization of interfaces to allow different components to communicate with each other. The implementation of standardized interfaces is implemented via ports that provide both functions for reading as well as for writing allowing data exchange (documentation).

Abstraction

CHROMOSOME possesses a hardware abstraction layer, which offers a platform-independent API. Thus, hardware specific functionalities are hidden from the application developer and in addition, it offers software services similar to a standard operating system.

The automated integration of different machinery requires a semantic and syntactic description of the services and functions the external machines offer. This allows the communication between different components without knowing details of each other. CHROMOSOME entails an explicit domain modelling tool which supports the user modelling a particular production setting (documentation).

Encountered forms of openness

The developed software architecture based on CHROMOSOME has the aim of both facilitating the integration of external machines as well as allowing developers to model applications. Integrating machines on the platform basically requires the external party to come up with a description of the services their machine offers.

As CHROMOSOME is also open source, it also allows customizing the software platform to domain-specific requirements.

Degree of openness

An analysis of the degree of openness and the associated business logic is constrained by the fact that CHROMOSOME constitutes a research project. Thus, there is so far not enough information available regarding its plans for commercialization. To provide a more detailed evaluation of appropriate degrees of openness of this platform, further exploration would be needed, e.g. by interviewing potential system adopters.

4.3 Cross-case analysis

This section provides the cross-case analysis comparing and analyzing differences and similarities across the different cases. This allows categorizing and clustering the results according to common patterns found across the different cases. The main focus of the cross-case analysis is to (1) explore and operationalize the notion of embedded system openness, and to explore (2) corresponding strategies for modularization.

4.3.1 Openness of embedded systems

One of the primary goals of the cases was to gain an operationalization of technical openness in embedded systems. This is in contrast to the last study, where the focus was on the organizational dimension of ES openness. The first approximation towards technical openness has been introduced in II.4.2., which based technical openness on the layer model of computer systems. The understanding of technical openness was further enriched in II.4.3 which discussed openness in light of the characteristics of ES (dependability, safety etc.). Classification according to the different layers of computer system holds validity in the light of the cases, but does not fully describe the different nuances of openness of ES. The cases reveal that technical openness for third-party innovation manifests itself quite differently in each of these cases. However, classification along the layer model does not sufficiently describe all kinds of openness encountered. The following paragraphs describe the different forms of technical openness, for third-party innovation, identified in the cases. They are ordered according to the level of access to a system regarding the layer model, but also go beyond the layer model:

Data openness: Users can access certain interfaces of the system, in order to collect system or process data, enabling them to build data-driven applications. This form of openness has, for example, been observed in the OpenXC case, the commercial vehicle platform as well as in the Prosyst E-Health Platform and the Qivicon case. The OpenXC case represents an environment with high safety requirements and RT constraints which is not jeopardized by data openness. Similar motivations can be found in the commercial vehicle case. The interview partner from the commercial vehicle case stated: *"Essentially, this utility vehicle is opened to allow for data access"*. In this example, data openness is implemented to allow additional services, like fleet management, which merely requires access to vehicle data. In the John Deere case, which features agricultural machinery, one of the primary use cases for data openness is to analyze data for crop management. This helps make crop planning more efficient. Many of these applications can also be based on historical data and do not necessarily have to reside on the ES itself. For instance, data-based services in the OpenXC case, can be run on an external device, such as a tablet PC. Thus, for data openness, ES providers often do not need to provide the same amount of resources.

Application openness: In contrast to data openness, application openness allows external applications not only to read data from the system, but also to change the behavior of the system. Application openness can be implemented to different degrees, with some ES already providing a fixed application core, which can be expanded at certain endpoints whereas others, like Qivicon, leave the most part of application development to externals. Prosyst's e-health middleware explicitly supports different degrees of application openness as the degree of openness can be determined by the systems provider building on the Prosyst platform: "*The firm who develops such a gateway on this base, of course controls, to what degree it should be opened*" (Interview Partner Prosyst Case).

For ES whose use cases have not been fully developed, or are subject to change, a high degree of application openness can account for uncertain customer demands. This applies especially when the opening firm does not want to take the risk of investing in additional applications, without having detailed knowledge about customer preferences ("*the interesting question is, in which direction the market will move [...] the same with the partners who will develop their first applications and become smarter in this process*", (Interview Qivicon)). This statement also demonstrates the value of application openness as an open innovation strategy.

Operating system openness: Openness on the OS layer means that users are allowed to make changes to the operating system, including switching to another OS itself. Often, the OS does not provide certain functionalities which are required for enabling additional applications. Qivicon, for example, allows external partners to integrate certain device standards, to broaden the range of supported devices on the platform. Additional device standards would therefore broaden the range of possible applications on top of the system.

In the case of the Kuka Youbot, users are also allowed to switch to another OS. In practice, this case is however more a theoretical option, as most users stick to the preinstalled Ubuntu Linux. In general, offfering externals the possibility to install their own OS also entails application openness, as the application layer directly builds on the OS layer.

Thus, operating system openness is rather a means of enabling application openness instead of pursuing it for its own sake. In the other cases, OS openness was not encountered, partly because of missing use cases but also due to RT and safety requirements.

Hardware openness: Hardware (HW) openness allows extending the existing HW base of an ES. Thus, firms typically allow the integration of complementary HW modules at the periphery of the system. An example of this is the John Deere case, where other firms can integrate additional implements to the tractors of John Deere. The hardware base, in this case the tractor, with its integrated ES, has not been opened for externals. As John Deere cannot supply the complete range of possible agricultural implements, they rely on specialized firms providing complementary additions to their tractors. *"The tractor constitutes the system base, whereas the actual function is delivered by the device connected to the tractors [...] which are supplied by other firms. John Deere also manufactures their own implements, but they cannot cover every niche."* The software integration takes place via the ISOBUS, already described in the application openness section. To a broader extent, this motivation is visible in the Qivicon case, where the integration of a broad spectrum of different devices on the Qivicon platform is rather essential: *"as an example, we also work on the integration of protocols, in particular radio-based protocols, to allow partners the integration of their devices."*

Hardware openness usually encompasses application openness as well, as it often entails allowing additional applications, which make use of the new hardware modules. Another insight gained by the cases, is that hardware openness often also implies application openness (as external parties would also develop additional applications, which make use of new hardware modules).

Table 12 classifies the cases according to the forms of openness of ES.

Table 12   Encountered forms of openness in cases

Case	Forms of openness	Openness description
Raspberry PI	Data openness, application openness, operating system openness, partial hardware openness	No defined use case by provider, therefore no particular restrictions on openness; general-purpose platform

Arduino	All forms of openness encountered	Due to open source and open hardware status no restrictions regarding openness; general-purpose platform
Google Glass	Data openness, application openness	Openness to allow externals to determine the main use cases of Google Glass; general-purpose platform
Project Ara	Data openness, application openness, hardware openness	Integration of additional software and hardware modules; general-purpose platform
SmartThings	Data openness, application openness, hardware openness	Openness for different hardware devices and software apps to enlarge ecosystem
LEGO Mindstorms	Data openness, application openness, hardware openness	Openness to allow users to determine the purpose of robotic platform
INCA	Application openness	Application development on open camera platform
Prosyst E-Health Middleware	Data openness, application openness, hardware openness	Integration of new hardware modules to the system; Development of SW applications using the existing hardware base
Infotainment System	Data openness, application openness	Use of vehicle data in combination with external data for additional applications; control certain functions via external devices;
John Deere	Data openness, application openness, hardware openness	SW integration of implements provided by third parties
Kuka Youbot	Data openness, application openness Operating	Additional hardware modules for robotics platform; SW development for robotics platform

	system openness, hardware openness	
Qivicon	Data openness, application openness, hardware openness	Integration of new hardware modules to the system; Development of SW applications on top
RACE Project	Application openness, hardware openness	Allow upgradability of hardware and software applications; add additional software functions
Commercial vehicle platform	Data openness	Access to vehicle data for fleet management, operations management, repair and maintenance
OpenXC	Data openness	Access to vehicle data to build additional applications on third-party devices
AutoPNP	Hardware openness	Facilitated integration of new HW components

4.3.2 Modularizing for openness

In the second part of the analysis, the impact of openness on the modularity of ES will be examined. The focus was especially to find out to what extent the characteristics of ES define potential modularizations when ES are opened. The inclusion of cases, which are highly subject to these characteristics, as well as of cases, which are less affected by these characteristics, is contributing to this aim.

Modularizing for data openness

Data openness has a rather small footprint in the overall architecture of a system. Basically, a firm needs to make sure that external users can only access certain data, without giving access to more confidential data. In addition the data access procedures themselves, should not compromise the system's proper functioning. The data-oriented applications themselves often run on external devices, for instance on mobile devices, like smart phone and tablet PCs. However, ES firms can also allow integration with the cloud. To realize this partitioning of data, access to it can be allowed via an additional data access layer. A common way to implement this is to add a module to the system. This module acts as a proxy for externals to control access to the data. This approach has for instance been chosen in the OpenXC platform, where the rest of the car's architecture remains unchanged. The device acting as the proxy, in the OpenXC platform, is the so-called "vehicle interface". According to the OpenXC specification, "it passively listens for a subset of CAN messages, performs required unit conversion or factoring and outputs a generic version to the USB interface." The vehicle interface only provides this particular function of translating the CAN messages, but additional applications are running outside this particular module. The separation of applications developed by users and the message definitions also increases IP protection and security, as e.g. reverse engineering is more difficult to accomplish. Similarly, the commercial vehicle case offers a central component of access for vehicle data. In contrast, John Deere realized the separation of data by implementing a secondary bus system, the so-called ISOBUS, a standardized bus system that can be used for communication between different system components. Both the OpenXC as well as the approach chosen in John Deere help to protect IP as well as to guarantee dependability and safety.

A modularization strategy to minimize costs and the impact on the original system is to outsource new applications outside the boundaries of the original system, e.g. by relying on mobile devices or a cloud infrastructure for additional applications. The OpenXC case uses this approach, where mobile devices act as the host for additional applications and at the same time provides the user interface for the applications. This strategy is especially applicable for data openness, as besides being able to access data, applications do not have strong dependencies to the system. In the infotainment case, we observed a similar strategy where new applications are streamed from the web and use the on-board display as a user interface.

Modularizing for application openness

In contrast to data openness, the footprint of application openness on the system is more pronounced, as ES must possess the capacity for additional applications. Commonly, ES are designed in accordance with pre-defined functions, which are not subject to change. To cater for additional applications, ES providers may need to re-modularize their systems. An example where this is particularly apparent is the INCA camera. Whereas the traditional camera architecture consists of a Field-Programmable Gate Array (FPGA), the INCA camera architecture is built on a SoC. This enables greater abstraction between hardware and software and therefore requires less knowledge of hardware from developers. According to the project leader of the INCA camera: *"we screened the market and realized, that we can use the core parts of smart-phones, so-called SOCs [....] they are cheaper, but also the development effort is smaller and at the same time, they offer more functionality."*

Running applications on the ES often constitutes a challenge. Many ES, which have been designated for a specific purpose, need to accommodate both for the core functions of an ES and for third-party applications. To achieve this, ES firms often partition their systems in separate domains for base functions and for third-party innovation. The main reason for separation is to ensure safety and RT requirements of the core functions. In the infotainment platform case, this allows "to bring innovation cycles known from the consumer industry to the infotainment domain". This is especially done, to protect safety-critical functions from being affected by additional applications. The separation of a system, in different parts, may also affect core interfaces of ES. As the John Deere case showed, the addition of a separate bus system (ISOBUS) provides a higher degree of freedom for additional third-party applications. On the one hand, the ISOBUS is less safety-critical than the CANBUS, which is used by the base vehicle functions. On the other hand, it allows a finer graduated control of openness by regulating access to the core parts of the system.

The isolation of critical parts can also be conducted gradually. The RACE project outlines two different paths towards achieving open architecture in the automotive domain, a revolutionary and evolutionary approach. Whereas both approaches would lead to the same architecture in the end, the evolutionary approach suggests a gradual isolation of critical parts. Thus, more and more critical parts would be isolated without taking too many risks.

Modularizing for operating system openness

Regarding operating system openness, modularization strategies for ES did not differ significantly from existing practices in general-purpose computer systems. However, the need to guarantee dependability and safety requirements emphasizes certain aspects. ES firms need to make sure that externals may not violate these constraints while making changes to the OS layer. For instance, Quivion realizes it by providing 'sandboxes' for additional OS modules, which isolates changes from the rest of the OS.

Modularizing for hardware openness

From a modularity perspective, enabling hardware openness for ES puts these systems closer to general-purpose systems (supporting heterogeneous hardware devices). This requires an additional middleware, or hardware abstraction layer, with the purpose of abstracting hardware details to developers. For instance, e-health platforms require interoperability with a large number of connectivity standards. Prosyst offers a specialized middleware for e-health platforms, which abstracts the details of various connection standards like Zigbee, Z-Wave etc. An additional advantage of using a middleware, is that software applications can be developed and tested independently of the target hardware, thus facilitating the development for externals (Fortiss 2011).

Platform providers integrating a diverse set of heterogeneous devices, such as Qivicon or Prosyst, offer a broad variety of different interface standards and protocols. To allow for the integration of devices, not conforming to existing standards, Qivicon leaves room for external developers to enhance the system with additional interface standards. The platform supports this by providing a "system sandbox", with enhanced permissions to implement these changes. Whereas systems like Prosyst and Qivicon need to conform to a broad variety of different connection standards. Other ES, like John Deere, follow a different approach concerning interfaces. The interface strategy of John Deere, with its ISOBUS, has already been discussed in the section "Modularizing for Application Openness". As the CANBUS constitutes a critical interface, the ISOBUS as a second bus system is used by external hardware providers to interact with other system components.

In Figure 13, the implications of the forms of openness on modularization are depicted. As it can be seen, operating system openness has the least implications regarding the modularity of the system.

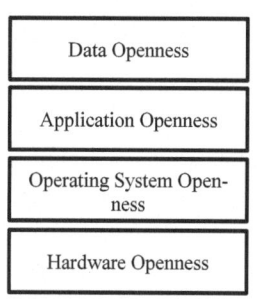

Data Openness	• Outsourcing of third-party applications to external devices • Data access via abstraction layer: e.g. proxy module or separate bus system
Application Openness	• Partitioning of execution environment for additional applications • Separation of bus systems to guarantee non-interference with critical system's functions
Operating System Openness	• provide limited access to OS, e.g. by sandbox approach
Hardware Openness	• Support for a broad variety of different standards • Abstraction from different connectivity standards and hardware details

Figure 13 Implications of openness of ES on modularity

A common modular approach in both data openness and application openness was the usage of partitioning. In data openness, outsourcing of third-party applications to external devices leads to a partitioned system. In application openness, the need to ensure the proper functioning of the device often leads to a certain partitioning of the system. In total, three forms of partitioning have been observed, which are depicted in table 13.

Table 13   Forms of partitioning

Partitioning of the execution environment	With this form of partitioning, ES providers can still keep their original architectures to a large extent. At the same time they can allow for openness on dedicated parts of their systems which expose general-purpose systems' characteristics
Partitioning of the key bus systems (providing interfaces for the different modules)	This partitioning is used, when the execution of additional applications takes place on the same execution environment, however, data transfer capacities of additional applications needs to be separated from the existing system functions
Partitioning by outsourcing additional applications on external devices	With this form of partitioning additional applications would run on external infrastructure like tablet PCs or smart phones, but also in the cloud. This can be done due to several reasons: (1) when running additional applications causes risks to the existing infrastructure, (2) to save costs (3) or if the necessary computing capabilities are not available on the original device. This approach is particularly applicable for data openness, but can also be pursued for some cases of application openness

4.4   Discussion of key findings

The first part of the findings presented different forms of ES openness and can partly be operationalized according to the layer model of embedded systems. However, in the analysis, an additional form of openness, namely data openness has been identified. Although similarly to application openness, it allows to build additional applications on top of the system, there are a couple of reasons to differentiate between these two forms of openness. First of all, applications which build on data openness do not change the behavior of the system and can thus be executed independently of the existing functionality of the ES. In addition, for ES providers the effort regarding modularization to implement data openness is rather low. To grant externals access to certain data, often an additional abstraction layer is introduced. The risks of violating the proper functioning of the ES are therefore limited. Data openness can thus be pursued as a first step to enable 'read-only' applications without having to invest too much effort and resources. The other forms of openness based on the layer model were application openness, operating system openness and hardware openness. All of these forms of openness are not mutually exclusive, but can also occur concurrently, as it has been seen in several of the explored cases.

Operating system openness played the least important role in the cases. This can be explained due to the role of the operating systems layer. With the operating systems layer providing access to the underlying hardware, there are seldom reasons for externals to make changes to this layer. However, sometimes, minor changes are needed, e.g. installing drivers for additional hardware devices.

Regarding the modularization of ES for open innovation, the findings show the following: A common theme which can be observed in the cases is a move towards a more clearly layered architecture, similar to general-purpose computer systems. Moving in this direction is however hindered by the technical characteristics of ES, in particular safety, security and RT requirements. Therefore, to allow for open innovation not just on the data level, firms often rely on partitioning of their system, which allows them to ensure these requirements.

Besides partitioning a system into parts with different degrees of openness, the design principles of abstraction and interface standardization are more pronounced when opening the ES. In order to also attract developers that do not possess domain knowledge of a specific ES, the ES providers are hiding the complexity via abstraction mechanisms. The need for interface standardization arises mainly to achieve compatibility and attract externals to contribute. Whereas a greater level of abstraction and interface standardization are already widely used in general-purpose systems, the need for partitioning is especially pronounced in open ES.

The required changes for openness in the modularity of ES also show that firms pursuing openness need to adapt a more complex system architecture in order to cater for different sets of requirements. This can in many cases lead to higher costs, as the systems need to offer enough capabilities to handle the additional workload but also to accommodate for different workload types. In terms of costs, data openness requires the least changes to the modularity of the system, thus causing fewer costs, whereas application openness in many cases requires major changes in the modularity of ES. The selection of a particular approach to modularize a system is therefore not only dependent on the technical characteristics of ES but is also informed by the resulting costs.

4.5   Conclusion and future perspectives

This study showed how technical systems such as embedded systems need to be modularized for open innovation. Furthermore, it offers an operationalization of the notion of openness in the context of ES. It can be seen, that pursuing openness in ES needs to take into account the technical characteristics of ES, and is also limited by it. In particular, it was shown, that openness is not only an organizational decision but involves considering technical constraints such as safety or real-time requirements. Considering these requirements also influences the modularization of ES, when opening them. The results also hold value for the platform literature, as they provide an in-depth perspective of the technical implications when firms are transforming their ES into a platform. Thus, it extends the notion of platform openness by taking a more technical view on the requirements of ES.

The study also holds managerial implications: It provides an overview of ES openness, which helps practitioners in pursuing ES openness and assessing the technical impact of openness due to its required changes in the modularity of the system. A limitation can be seen in the number of cases: to provide more details regarding the different industries, a higher amount of cases would need to be elicited. Further on, a more detailed exploration of the influence of other factors on the modularity of ES, such as legal or costs aspects would be interesting. In this regard, an interesting research path would be to show how ES firms can gradually re-modularize their system to more openness. The RACE case with its focus on an evolutionary approach towards modularity for openness already constitutes an example. Re-modularizing a system towards more openness also holds implications for the industry structure as a such. Firms opening a system would not only open their systems technically, but need to take into account the organizational industry structure at the same time. Another limitation of this study is that it only involved cases of ES, which are opened or are in the opening process. Further studies could for instance target ES, which cannot be opened for open innovation in order to explore the boundaries of openness in ES.

5   Study 4 - Open innovation without opening ES

The following study deals with open innovation in ES, which are not specifically opened for open innovation. Thus, it differs from the preceding studies, which were focusing on open innovation where firms are actively opening ES. Although it is essential for firms to open their ES to implement an open innovation strategy, it does not capture the whole spectrum of open innovation taking place. In order to benefit from the full spectrum of OI, firms also need to consider OI, which occurs outside the domain they explicitly opened to their customers. As it has been described in II.3., this refers to ES where the ES provider did not plan for open innovation or where open innovation occurs at unexpected parts of the system. As such cases are usually unforeseen by the ES provider, this study aims to provide cases as exemplary showcases. Although designing their systems for such unexpected cases of OI is challenging for ES firms, understanding these cases would help ES firms to improve their approach towards open innovation. Therefore, the underlying research question of this study is *"What forms of OI can be found without opening ES?"*. Thus, the focus of this study is rather classifying these occurrences of open innovation instead of exploring ways how they can be enabled.

5.1 Research design

The research method applied to this study is based on mini case studies, also referred to as case vignettes. It follows a holistic multiple case study design as outlined by Yin, (2008), providing more generalizability by obtaining contrasting or replicating results. It allows to explore a phenomenon in depth, in the context in which it occurs and where the boundaries between phenomenon and context cannot be clearly determined. The decision for mini case studies instead of larger case studies has been chosen as the observed phenomenon is limited in scope: it does not focus on required design decisions taken by the ES provider to open their systems, rather it describes situations where OI took place without the providers' preparatory decision towards openness. Nonetheless, a mini case study design allows to explain why a particular phenomenon took place.

5.1.1 Data Collection

The selection of the cases was accomplished by following a theoretical sampling strategy. According to this sampling strategy, cases are selected to replicate existing cases or to extend emergent theory, but also in order to fill theoretical categories and to select examples of polar types (Eisenhardt 1989). In the study at hand, the goal was to select polar cases, which allow to uncover the distinct categories of the explored phenomenon. Due to the scattered occurrence of the phenomenon to-be-analyzed, the mini cases were identified by multiple internet sources. Partly the cases have been encountered by reviewing popular online technical magazines such as endgadget.com or techcrunch.com. Other cases were identified via reviewing different blogs, which cover hardware and software hacks by users or deal with user innovation with embedded devices in general. This approach was taken because open innovation without opening ES is a phenomenon which does not occur in specific industries but takes place sporadically and is also not always reported in research or media. Data collection took place between April and June 2015. In total eight different mini cases have been discovered which are summarized in Table 14.

Table 14   Cases overview

Case	Case description
Sony attachable smart phone camera	Object lens released by Sony which can be attached to different smart phones
Prynt	Smart phone add-on allowing to print photos stored on the smart phone
Microsoft Kinect	Sensor device used for video gaming which was hacked for different use cases
Sony PlayStation PS 3	Gaming console which was used for building a supercomputing cluster
Beep	External module which transforms speakers into streaming media players
Garageio	Smart phone integration for garage door systems
LEGO Mindstorms	Originally closed toy robotic platform which was extended by external users
Xbox Media Center	Game console which was hacked to allow usage as a media center

The sources used for the mini cases are depicted in Table 15.

Table 15   Sources for cases

Case	Sources
Sony attachable smart phone camera	http://www.sonymobile.com/global-en/products/accessories/dsc-qx100/ http://www.engadget.com/2013/09/18/sony-qx10-review/
Prynt	http://www.itmagazine.ch/Artikel/58515/Aus_Smartphone_wird_Polaroid-Kamera.html https://www.kickstarter.com/projects/prynt/prynt-the-first-instant-camera-case-for-iphone-and
Microsoft Kinect	http://www.bbc.com/news/technology-11742236 http://www.nytimes.com/2012/06/03/magazine/how-kinect-spawned-a-commercial-ecosystem.html?pagewanted=all&_r=0
Sony PlayStation PS 3	http://www.nytimes.com/2014/12/23/science/an-economical-way-to-save-progress.html?_r=0.
Beep	http://www.nbcnews.com/tech/gadgets/music-your-ears-new-gadget-turns-dumb-speakers-smart-n23051 https://www.thisisbeep.com/
Garageio	https://garageio.com/ http://www.digitaltrends.com/home/garageio-make-dumb-garage-door-smart/
LEGO Mindstorms	http://www.ideaconnection.com/open-innovation-success/Lego-Success-Built-on-Open-Innovation-00258.html http://library.fora.tv/2008/04/08/MITs_Eric_von_Hippel_Open_Innovation

| Xbox Media Center | http://hackerinnovation.mikepinder.co.uk/index.php/Product_Innovations_De-signed_to_be_Hacked http://techcrunch.com/2014/08/01/12-years-after-its-debut-on-hacked-xboxes-xbmc-changes-its-name-to-kodi/ |

5.1.2 Analysis

After identifying the mini cases, they have been subsequently analyzed. From the identified sources, the relevant text passages have been extracted and summarized by paraphrasing the individual statements. By comparing and contrasting different cases to each other, different categories of open innovation without openness were derived. The analysis was informed by theory on modularity as it has been outlined in II.4.5. In particular, the principles of modularization according to Baldwin & Clark (2000) have been used as a framework to categorize the different forms of OI. These were the principles of abstraction, information hiding and partitioning as well as standardization of interfaces.

The categories represent different approaches towards extending an ES by externals where the ES providers did not offer dedicated point of extensions by opening their systems. Moreover, the reaction of the ES provider has also been analyzed to describe possible strategies form firms to benefit from unforeseen OI. However, this was not observable in every case.

5.2   Open innovation by the creation of new interfaces

The first type of open innovation encountered in the cases can be described by its underlying mechanism: the creation of new interfaces by externals. In this approach, the enhancement of the ES is dependent on an extension point of the system, which is not yet present. In order to build additional use cases, the external innovator first of all had to create an additional interface serving as an extension point. Thus, the innovators needed to enhance the degree of modularity for the implementation of their innovation. In total, four cases have been found where this has been implemented. They will be described in the following paragraphs.

Beep

Beep is a Wi-Fi module which can be connected to a speaker system in order to stream music from a smart phone. Thus, Beep is acting as an interface for providing Wi-Fi capabilities to an otherwise internet-less device. The module is connected via the aux-in port of the speaker. Although a speaker is itself not an embedded system, but rather a component that can be used as part of a larger system, the module allows extending the use of the original speakers. Thus, the speakers can be integrated in a system, which would not be possible without the Beep module.

In terms of open innovation, the original speakers were simpler components, which would be directly connected to e.g. a PC, but did not itself constitute an independent system. By the use of Beep, these components are enhanced to a fully embedded system. The Beep module can be seen as an interface, which allows to broaden the use cases of the original speakers.

Sony - Smart phone attachable lens-style camera

This case describes an object lens released by Sony that can be attached to a smart phone with a special adapter matching to the particular smart phone. Whereas the adapter can be used to physically attach the object lens to the smart phone, the software integration is achieved by using near-field communication (NFC) which represents a wireless way to exchange data. Thus, the smart phone can be used as the camera base in order to take pictures and save them on the smart phone but also to use the smart phone's display to view them.

From an open innovation perspective, this enhancement of a smart phone is an example where innovation took place on a level, which was not foreseen by the smart phone producer. Although a smart phone offers diverse software interfaces, it is usually designed as a single device, which is not enhanced by additional hardware parts. Therefore, it does not offer a dedicated hardware interface that can be used by Sony. By creating the adapter, Sony essentially created the interface in order to come up with a complementary innovation. Therefore, this case is different to platforms, where external innovators would rely on the interfaces provided by the ES firm.

Prynt - Photo printer for smart phone

Prynt is a start-up company, which produces a photo printer module which can be directly attached to a smart phone allowing to immediately print out copies of pictures made with the smart phone. Thus, Prynt follows a similar approach once pioneered by Polaroid. Similar to the attachable camera case described before, Prynt is also creating a physical interface that couples a smart phone with its printer module. To exchange data, it can either use the "lightning connector" in the case of connecting it to an iPhone by Apple, or the micro-USB interface of Android smart phones.

Garageio

Garageio provides the possibility to remotely steer existing garage door opening systems. These systems often do not offer a remote control that can be used to open or close the garage door. For that reason, Garageio developed a device, which can be installed to an existing garage opening system. This device can then be steered via a Wi-Fi connection. Thus, a smart phone can be used to control the garage door via the home Wi-Fi network. Wi-Fi as a technology standard has the additional advantage that the device can be monitored or controlled not only in the immediate proximity of the door, but also from other locations as well. The device also offers a web-based dashboard which users can access to monitor their garage doors

To extend a garage door with the Garageio module, a control wire needs to be plugged in to the existing garage opening system. Garageio provides a list of garage door openers that are compatible to their system. In contrast to the preceding cases, the role of the hardware interface is less pronounced in the Garageio case. There is necessity to physically attach the Garageio module to the garage opening system.

Although the garage door opening systems already provide an interface which Garageio makes use of, these systems have not been explicitly opened for open innovation. Garageio similarly to the Beep case uses an already existing interface, but wraps it with an additional interface providing Wi-Fi connectivity.

5.3   Open innovation by hacking

The second type of open innovation without opening ES found in the cases resolves around hacking the original ES. By hacking, innovators were able to change the device according to their needs. In total, four of the cases elicited in this study fall under this category. The next paragraphs describe each of these cases.

Microsoft Kinect

The Kinect by Microsoft is an embedded system equipped with motion sensors allowing to register the movements of persons interacting with the Kinect. Initially, the Kinect was designed to work together with the Xbox game console. Shortly after the release of the

Kinect, the electronic kit maker sparked a contest offering $3.000 for successfully coming up with control software to get access to the functionalities of the Kinect. Thus, it is possible to connect other devices and interact with the Kinect. Although Microsoft was at the beginning condoning this practice, they later realized that it spawned a great variety of use cases, which they did not plan for. In the beginning of 2012, at the International Consumer Electronics Show, the then appointed CEO of Microsoft, Steve Ballmer, announced a specific version of the Kinect which would work together with other devices than the Xbox. Microsoft saw the potential of using the Kinect for other use cases, which would increase the sales volume. The goal of Microsoft was to spawn an ecosystem around their Kinect.

Sony PlayStation PS3

The Sony PlayStation has been developed to play video games and thus constitutes a more special-purpose built computer system then regular PCs or notebooks. However, under its hood it has the same components, which are also used for general-purpose systems and thus would also suffice for other use cases. Furthermore, as video games are rather demanding in performance, they offer a high level of computing capabilities. Due to its relatively cheap price ($250 - $300), they have been chosen by Gaurav Khanna from the University of Massachusetts to form the base of a supercomputer. Sony also allowed its users for the PS3 to install their own operating system, facilitating the deviant use of the PS3. In 2010, the supercomputer lab already included 1716 consoles. In contrast to the Microsoft Kinect case, the PS3 did not have to be hacked for this unforeseen use case. However, it follows a similar approach in using a system not for its expected use case.

LEGO Mindstorms

LEGO Mindstorms constitutes a robotics learning platforms mainly targeting children and beginners who would like to make the first steps towards working with robotics. It offers a programmable platform allowing users to build their own robots based on a predefined set of LEGO bricks, sensors, actuators and motors. Each of these components are programmable allowing the users to build their own robotics applications. However, the number of functions and the extensibility of the LEGO Mindstorms platform were limited as LEGO kept its platform proprietary.

After the platform was released on the market, it became popular in a short time frame. In the first three weeks after market launch, over a 1000 advanced users in a web-coordinated campaign were already hacking the platform. (Idea Connection).

As a reaction to the hacking of their platform, LEGO introduced the LEGO factory, a web platform allowing users to design their own Lego Mindstorms packages. In addition, in the next version of LEGO Mindstorms, LEGO included user-developed parts which were included as part of the platform.

The LEGO case gives an example of a company, which realized the potential of open innovation which was not planned for by the ES provider. They actively embraced the emerging community and thus were able to profit from unintended open innovation.

Xbox Media Center (XBMC)

The Xbox Media Center (XBMC) denotes a software platform running on the hacked Xbox game console. In 2002, the Microsoft Xbox was hacked to allow users to not only use the Xbox as a media center, but also to use it as a media player for music and video content. In its original form, the Xbox did not support these different use cases. Gradually, a large community grew around the platform with a growing amount of functionality. The hacker project later also became independent of the Xbox and was established as an open source platform running on all kinds of platforms.

This case is very similar to the hack of the Microsoft Kinect, as it also resolves around a hardware platform with the potential to support different software applications as originally intended by the hardware provider.

5.4 Discussion

This study encountered two different forms of open innovation without opening ES: OI through the creation of new interfaces by externals and OI by hacking. In both forms of openness, the underlying ES have not been designed for these complementary innovations. In the following, both of these forms will be discussed:

Unintended open innovation by the creation of new interfaces

In the first form, the underlying system did not yet possess the interface, which was necessary to implement certain additional use cases. In both the Prynt and the Sony case, the physical interface to integrate an additional module to the system was missing. The physical interface is used to attach the additional module to the existing system. The software integration of the additional modules in both these cases is achieved via already existing interfaces, in both cases by the wireless Bluetooth standard. Although the creation of an additional hardware interface was not absolutely necessary for the proper functioning of the enhancement, it plays a vital role. Its value proposition is the additional convenience the extended solution offers.

The Garageio and the Beep case were also resolving around the creation of an additional interface. In contrast to the preceding two cases, the additional interface is essential for the possibility of the corresponding value propositions. In these cases, the aim of the created interface is to enable communication with a different system. In both these cases, the original system was integrated with a smart phone, but different types of systems would also be conceivable.

Unintended open innovation by hacking

Regarding open innovation by hacking, the system already had the capabilities needed for the additional use cases; however, they were closed for external developers. Thus, the original device already had the potential to harbor additional applications. The Xbox, the Sony PlayStation and the Kinect case have been unchanged in terms of its hardware foundation. Rather, the devices have been hacked to execute different software or changing the existing software platform. In contrast, the Lego Mindstorms platform was hacked in order to allow the integration of additional, external hardware modules, such as sensors. However, in each of these cases, hacking the underlying software platform was the prerequisites.

From a firm's perspective, hacking the device may not always be undesirable. ES like Lego Mindstorms are not subject to safety or security characteristics. Thus, the damage to the company's reputation is rather limited. Therefore, the ES company can even benefit from the additional use cases provided by externals. In both the Kinect and the Lego Mindstorms, the companies perceived the potential arising due to open innovation. Firms thus may spawn new business models for their systems (Kinect case) or they may benefit by further sales opportunities (Lego Mindstorms).

Comparison with existing OI practices

From an OI perspective, both of these two described forms of unintended OI fall under the view of OI as advocated by von Hippel. This view has been presented in the theoretical part (II.3). In addition, in this part, the perception of products as use-generative goods (Brown 2013) has been presented. Similar to that notion, the cases presented in this study represent systems, which were used in ways not anticipated by the ES provider. The present study operationalizes this notion in the ES field and shows the practices which are employed by externals to transform ES into use-generative goods. In both discovered forms, the conditions to allow the use of the ES in novel ways had to be generated by the external party (either by hacking or by the creation of new interfaces).

5.5 Conclusion

Although in each of these cases, open innovation was unanticipated for the ES provider, firms can nonetheless learn from it. By analyzing the cases, it was shown, that OI in this setting, although unforeseen, can be divided in different categories. Basically, there are two forms of unforeseen OI: OI by the *creation of new interfaces* and *by hacking*. Whereas the creation of new interfaces extends the system with the necessary prerequisites for a particular innovation, OI by hacking enforces an opening of the system which has otherwise already the capabilities for OI. An additional conclusion which can be drawn from the cases is that the technical characteristics of ES which would hinder OI are absent in these cases. None of these cases was to a large degree affected by RT-constraints or safety requirements. In some of the cases, although initially open innovation took place without openness, the ES providers were starting to open their system after they realized the potential of the external contributions. This also points to opportunities for further research. Whereas this study focuses on the circumstances under which unforeseen OI takes place, further studies could analyze strategies of firms to incorporate those OI initiatives as part of their OI strategy. Especially in the case of *OI by hacking*, firms could proactively try to incorporate that as part of their OI strategy. Thus, it can be seen, that the two forms of OI analyzed in this thesis, OI without opening ES and opening ES for OI are not completely separable phenomena. Rather, unforeseen OI can blend into OI pursued by the ES provider.

The study also has limitations: due to the comparatively low sample size, the results offer first insights in the phenomenon of OI without opening, but can be generalize only to a limited degree. As the data collection relied on popularized cases mostly from internet sources, the choice of cases is limited. To come up with more generalizable results, a broader study design could for instance been achieved by directly surveying a larger number of ES firms. This would allow to identify additional cases of open innovation without openness and to get more details about the setting in which it took place.

Part IV

Discussion

1   Reflection on the studies' results

The preceding part encompassed the empirical studies of this thesis answering the research questions, which have been laid out in the research design chapter (III.1). Each of these research questions constitutes a part of the overall research question of this thesis. In this chapter, the aim is to discuss the contribution of the individual studies to the main research question of this thesis. Furthermore, the limitations of each of the studies and the studies' design will be discussed.

To draw synergies from the different empirical studies, Chapter 2 presents a cross-study discussion. Whereas the individual studies were focusing on a particular aspect of open innovation in embedded systems, the results also have implications on the other studies' results. However, as the results of the individual studies have some overlap with the other studies, there is potential for refining and comparing the other studies' results. Furthermore, it also allows to draw additional conclusions.

First of all, there will be a summary of the research questions of this thesis and how each of the individual studies contributes to answer the main research question. The main research question of this thesis was:

"How can Open Innovation be enabled for ES?"

The research question assumes that firms actively need to enable open innovation before it takes place. Firms accomplish this via opening their ES for externals. The first three studies explored different facets of open innovation through the opening of ES. To answer the main research question, it was necessary to show in what regard open innovation for ES differs from open innovation in general. Therefore, the first study dealt with the following research question: *"How do the technical characteristics of ES influence open innovation processes*? (first study).

As ES have specific characteristics which constrains the potential for opening them for open innovation, this study's aim was to explore their impact on potential open innovation processes. Based on the literature, it was shown, that conducting open innovation for ES requires simultaneously opening the organization as well as the ES itself.

As a research method, a conceptual study has been conducted which was based on existing literature both in the field of ES as well as OI. One reason for this approach was that to my current knowledge, the existing body of literature did not yet try to bring together these two topics. Therefore, contrasting both streams of literature to each other is a promising approach to derive additional knowledge. Furthermore, contrasting these two bodies of research also facilitates to identify the gap in the literature. The study provided the foundation for an in-depth exploration of both the organizational and technical perspective of openness addressed in second and third study.

The second study of this thesis dealt with the required organizational opening of ES firms to enable open innovation. ES firms opening both their organization as well as their ES for OI have to consider various risks resulting from the technical opening. These risks involve both technical factors (e.g. safety or RT constraints) as well as organizational risks (e.g. IP protection or liability issues). The underlying research question of the second study therefore was: *"How can firms pursue the opening of their systems and their organizations to enable open innovation?"* (Study 2). For this study, an expert-interview approach has been chosen. Although the individual expert interviews did not tackle particular cases of openness in ES, all of the experts were involved in one or more projects where ES have been opened. The selection of experts from various field of the ES industries also contributed to the generalizability of the results. The results presented different forms of organizational openness and how they are influenced by technical and organizational factors. Regarding the main research question, organizational openness represents one main aspect of how firms enable OI in ES. It could be further enriched by taking a combined perspective on technical and organizational forms of openness would. The cross-study discussion following in the next chapter will address this aspect.

Whereas the third study was thus focusing on the organizational openness required for ES, the third fourth was focusing on openness on a technical level. It answered the following research question: *How can embedded systems be technically opened to enable open innovation?*

The literature on platforms and modularity has shown, that opening an ES for open innovation also requires modularizing the ES accordingly. Modularization is a way to achieve partial openness, which allows keeping certain parts closed while opening other parts dependent on the openness strategy. Therefore, modularity theory was the theoretical perspective applied in this multiple case study. To answer the research question, it was necessary to examine actual ES, which have been opened for open innovation. Thus it was explored how these systems were opened and how system designers modularized their systems to achieve the desired degree of openness. In retrospection, the multiple case study approach turned out to be an adequate approach to answer the research question of this study. In particular, it allowed including a large variety of different cases of embedded systems in the study. It would have been further beneficial to increase the number of interviews. However, as the topic of technical openness also constitutes a strategic value for many ES providers which is partly confidential, data collection was therefore constrained.

The first three studies focused on OI enabled by opening ES. However, OI can also take place without opening ES. To illuminate the phenomenon of OI in ES comprehensively, it was also necessary to explore OI in ES where ES are not explicitly opened. Exploring both forms of OI in ES also allows evaluating the implications of opening an ES in more detail, by contrasting it with open innovation without openness. Therefore, in the empirical part (Part III), the fourth study dealt with OI without opening the underlying ES (III, 6). The study was based on eight cases of ES which have not been specifically opened. By categorizing these cases, the phenomenon of OI without opening and its underlying mechanisms were illuminated. Although the ES firm initially does not play an active role in this form of OI, considering it allows ES firms to enhance their OI strategy. Some of the cases in the fourth study also showed how the firms incorporated these user-driven innovation initiatives into their OI strategy. This led to the conclusion that firms can further enhance their open innovation strategy by incorporating the OI initiatives not enabled by opening ES. The difference between these two forms of OI in ES will further be discussed in the cross-study discussion in the next chapter.

Regarding the limitations of the fourth study, a larger number of cases would still have the potential to provide more in-depth results. However, the main focus of this thesis was on the first form of OI in ES, namely OI by opening ES.

Another aspect which can be derived from the main research question (*"How can Open Innovation be enabled for ES?"*) is the combined perspective of both organizational as well as technical opening of ES. Both of these two perspectives have been explored in this thesis, namely in the second and the third study of this thesis. However, answering the overall research question can benefit from contrasting the results from the individual studies to each other. The cross-study discussion in the following chapter will contribute towards achieving this aim.

In a broader sense, enabling open innovation could also include issues like the additional support ES providers would give external developers. However, this was not included as a separate study, as the topic of providing tools for externals has already been extensively covered in other works, e.g. in the literature on toolkits for open innovation. Furthermore, opening the ES for open innovation more clearly takes the role of an enabler, whereas supplying toolkits would rather qualify as facilitators for open innovation.

2   Cross-Study discussion

Although each of the research questions addresses different aspects of open innovation in ES, the results of the four conducted studies also have implications on the other studies as well. In the present chapter, the four studies of this thesis will be frequently referred to by their number. For an easier reading of the present chapter, the following listing summarizes the studies in this thesis:

- **Study 1**: Conceptual study on the applicability of the three core OI processes in ES
- **Study 2**: Study on organizational openness for OI in ES
- **Study 3**: Study on technical openness for OI in ES
- **Study 4**: Empirical study on OI without opening ES

With regard to the different studies in this thesis, a cross-study discussion has the potential to refine the results in the following ways:

- Providing a clearer picture of the differences and commonalities between the two fundamental forms of OI in ES covered in this thesis: the results of the first study which dealt with *OI in ES without opening* can be contrasted with the results of the other three studies

- The second and the third study, which were based on empirical data, can be used for comparison with the findings of the first study. The first study brought together the two literature streams of embedded systems and open innovation and was therefore conceptual in nature. By reflecting on its results in light of the subsequent two empirical studies, its findings can be reexamined and complemented.

- The findings of the second study regarding the organizational openness of ES can be contrasted to the cases in the third study. First of all, this allows to show which form of organizational openness the firms in the cases have chosen. This also allows to examine the applicability of the three forms of organizational openness which were presented in the second study. Secondly, the case data also allows a better understanding of the different forms of organizational openness. Analyzing the cases regarding to the chosen form of organizational openness allows to gain

an increased understanding what factors were crucial for their chosen degree of
openness.

A graphical summary of the cross-study discussion, which will be performed in this part,
is given in Figure 14.

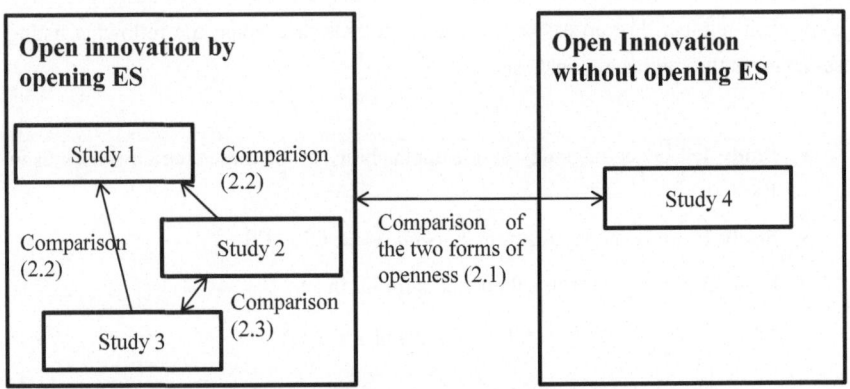

Figure 14 Outline of the cross-study discussion

2.1   Comparison of the two forms of OI in ES

In this thesis, it has been differentiated between two different forms of OI in ES: *open
innovation without opening ES* and *OI by opening ES.* Although these two forms of OI
have different preconditions, the mechanisms how OI takes place are similar.

From a technical point of view, these two approaches have similar requirements regarding modularity. Both of these approaches are only feasible for ES, which already possess
a sufficient degree of general-purpose orientation. This can be seen as the innovators in
the cases presented from study 4 did not change the original architecture of the underlying ES. Rather, they were able to break in an existing system (OI by hacking) or they
augmented the system (creation of new interfaces) and therefore extended the system.
However, the technical requirements for OI in ES, that have been found in the third study,
have already been present. *OI by hacking* takes place in a system, which already builds
on a modular architecture allowing the extension of the system. Regarding *OI by the
creation of new interfaces,* the add-on by the innovators could also take place in a system
that has been opened for OI. This example shows that systems are often to some degree
implicitly open, although the ES provider might not intend this. This discussion seems

to suggest, that technically, the difference between these two forms of openness is negligible. However, the cases elicited in the first study do not represent the full spectrum of closed ES. Rather they represent individual cases where the technical requirements for OI are already present to some degree.

In these cases, the difference between these two forms of openness is rather based on organizational decisions towards openness. ES firms face the challenge of selecting the right approach how to deal with unforeseen OI: First of all, they need to evaluate the potential of unforeseen OI and decide whether they would like to foster these approaches. Secondly, they would need to find a strategy how to incorporate unforeseen OI in their open innovation strategy. Dealing with unforeseen OI in ES also represents an interesting avenue for further research. Whereas research on open innovation, especially reflected in von Hippel's view on OI already offers a wide body of literature, it does not yet deal specifically with ES.

2.2   Implications of study 2 and 3 on the results of study 1

One limitation mentioned in the first study was that its results were solely based on a conceptual analysis but did not have empirical backing. However, the second and the third study help to refine the results gathered in this study. The first study discussed the applicability of the three core OI processes in ES. As the second and the third study dealt with the Outside-In process, they only allow the comparison with the findings relating to the Outside-In process in the first study. Table 16 shows the original results concerning the Outside-In process from the first study. It shows how the different characteristics of ES affect the Outside-In process.

Table 16   Implications of the ES characteristics on the outside-in process (Results of the first study)

ES characteristic	Outside-In Process
Dependability	Dependability more difficult to ensure with high modularity; Safety requirements limit licensing possibilities
Efficiency	Aim of cost efficiency could better be attained by outside licensing
Sensors and actuators	External know-how could be beneficial for sensors and actuators due to high knowledge intensity
Real-time constraints	Design for modularity needs to ensure real-time constraints, e.g. by tight coordination with partners
Reactive systems	*no implications found*

Hybrid systems	Higher knowledge intensity due to dichotomy of HW and SW, which could be met by external know how; Physical constraints hinder separate, modular design
Dedicated user interface	*no implications found*
Dedicated towards a specific application	*no implications found*

Especially the results gained from the second and third study allow to refine the conceptually derived results. This analysis however does not claim completeness, as the cases were not specifically conducted to empirically validate the findings from the second study. Nonetheless, they can complement these results. The next paragraphs discusses the implications, which can be drawn from the empirical studies for each of the ES characteristics in Table 16.

Dependability and real-time constraints

The role of dependability characteristics and real-time constraints in limiting openness has largely been confirmed by the cases. The empirical studies elaborated how these characteristics can be considered when opening ES. In particular, the role of modularity to handle these characteristics has been explored. Regarding the question, whether dependability is more difficult to ensure with higher modularity, the cases do not provide unambiguous results. On the one hand, systems are often designed in an integral way to ensure the close cooperation among different parts of a system. On the other hand, modularity helps to partition the system into critical and on-critical parts. In any case, modularity is seen as a strategy to harmonize openness requirements with the need for dependability. In particular, it has been seen, that modularizing systems in such a way, that critical parts are isolated, is a strategy used by ES providers. In contrast to the benefits of modularity, in the second study it was also pointed out that modularity comes with higher risks as failures can often be found at interface of logically correct components (Saglietti 2004). For this argument, no specific empirical evidence was found.

Another observation from the cases was, that the presence of higher dependability requirements leads to a closer cooperation with external partners. Especially in the automotive domain, new applications would only become part of the system when the automotive firm approves them. The same conclusion does not hold for the cases where the applications do not touch critical parts, such as what has been observed in the OpenXC case (also dealing with automotive ES) which features only data openness.

The presence of dependability requirements such as safety also requires ES firms to certify their solutions, including the solutions provided by partners. An example is the e-health industry, which requires the accomplishment of certain certification procedures and thus tighter coordination efforts with partners. The second study came to similar conclusions, where firms with higher dependability requirements are more likely to pursue network openness instead of market openness. However, it is not always possible to clearly distinguish the different aspects of dependability (safety, reliability, maintainability or availability), as they often occur simultaneously.

The cases showed that the presence of real-time characteristics has also been a constraint. To still conduct open innovation, firms modularize their systems in such a way, that the real-time affected parts are isolated form the opened parts.

Reactive systems

For the characteristics of ES being reactive systems, the empirical studies did not find any implications on the outside-in process.

Efficiency

Concerning the characteristic of efficiency, it can be observed that pursuing openness in ES is met with a trade-off concerning efficiency. To ensure that a variety of different applications can be executed on a particular device, there are existing system capabilities needed which was also observed in the cases. This leads to higher costs but also to higher energy needs.

Hybrid systems

The characteristic of hybrid systems refers to the dichotomy of HW and SW parts in ES. In the first study, it was stated that the complexity, which comes with increasing functionalities, can be easier handled by relying on external know-how. This reflects one of the goals of OI in ES, which has also been confirmed in the cases. However, empirical evidence also suggests that ES firms themselves reduce the complexity of their systems in order to facilitate external development. The primary mechanism to achieve that goal is to modularize their system to hide complexity.

Sensors and actuators

Regarding the presence of sensors and actuators, similar conclusions can be made than for the characteristic of 'hybrid systems. Sensors and actors are in fact one example of the physical parts of ES, which are often contributed to by externals when firms are pursuing open innovation in the hardware realm.

Dedicated user interfaces

Concerning dedicated user interfaces, empirical evidence shows that open ES are rather moving to already existing, standardized user interfaces. In many cases, the opened ES is controlled by smart phones or tablets. The move to rely on smart phones or tablets as the primary user interface is motivated both by convenience for the user as well as by cost arguments.

Dedication towards a specific application

This characteristic loses its significance for opened ES, as they naturally would allow additional applications not perceived during design time.

In summary, the results from the conceptual study have been largely confirmed by the empirical data. In particular, the empirical data allowed to operationalize the implications of the ES characteristics on the Outside-In process. Furthermore, the empirical studies showed how to tackle the challenges arising from these characteristics, e.g. by specifically modularizing the system for openness. Another observation was that some of the characteristics of ES lose relevance in the context of OI and therefore do not influence the outside-in process. Especially, the characteristics of 'dedicated user interfaces' and 'dedicated towards a specific application' are often not observable anymore in open ES.

2.3   Implications of the third studies' cases on the second study

The following section deals with the implications of the cases elicited in the third study on the results of the second study.

In this thesis, two different perspectives on openness in ES have been considered: openness from an organizational point of view and openness from a technical point of view. The second study was concerned with exploring the different forms of organizational openness related to openness of ES. It resulted in three different forms of organizational openness when opening ES: internal openness and two forms of external openness (network openness and market openness). These forms of organizational openness are once more depicted in Figure 15.

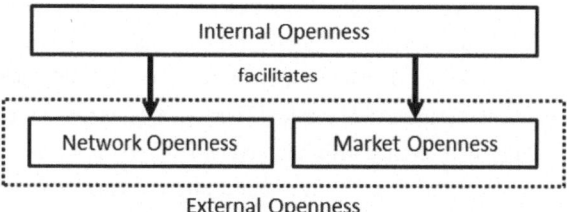

Figure 15 Organizational forms of ES openness

Based on these three forms of organizational openness, the next section shows which forms of organizational openness have occurred in the fourth studies' cases. Furthermore, additional findings, which either complement or enrich the results from the third study will be presented. In particular, it will be shown whether the encountered forms of organizational openness can also be found in practice and how ES companies are implementing them.

Encountered forms of organizational openness in the third studies' cases

Whereas the focus in the cases of the third study was on technical openness, they also allowed to observe the forms of organizational openness depicted in Figure 15. Most cases possess either market openness or network openness, with internal openness being only visible in one case. However, it cannot be derived from the cases that internal openness is only a marginal form of openness. First of all, case selection did not systematically try to include cases with internal openness. Furthermore, cases, which possess external openness, are more visible from an external perspective as firms release more information about it. In contrast, internal openness refers to firms that design their system in a more open way but not necessarily due to openness for externals. Rather, they pursue internal openness to gain more flexibility for further use cases of their system.

Implications of the case study results on internal openness

Internal openness has been mainly implemented when the ES firms wanted to capture the profits resulting from additional applications on top of an ES itself. The commercial vehicle case was solely focusing on internal openness without allowing externals to extend the platform. Similarly, the infotainment was mostly relying on internal openness although also partly relied on network openness. In the second study, one result was that internal openness and external openness resemble each other from a technical point of view. The results in the third studies' cases provide further evidence for this result. For instance, the modularization in the commercial vehicle case, which features internal openness, would also be sufficient for external openness. In the infotainment case, the re-modularization was pursued to realize faster innovation cycles internally, although it would also allow for enhancements from outside parties. These two examples indicate that technically, there is not so much difference between modularizing for internal openness as for external openness. However, there is also contrasting evidence. The John Deere Case was for instance relying on a separate bus system for external enhancements. Thus, it is possible to minimize risks that would otherwise endanger the proper functioning of the system. In case of internal openness, separating these bus systems would not be as important. As the system provider would decide himself on future enhancements, potential risks could be easier evaluated. This case shows that the presence of safety or RT-constraints would require additional consideration in the modularization for external openness.

In the INCA case, internal openness is applied partially. Customizations which require changing certain system functions are done by Fraunhofer itself, whereas additional applications which do not require making changes on lower layers can be achieved by externals. These changes on lower layers would also require additional know-how to accomplish. The INCA case showed that to fulfill certain tasks like integrating an additional sensor, certain changes at lower system layers would need to be performed. These changes would concern the operating system layer and the Ducati layer which is underneath the OS layer. These changes would be made by Fraunhofer directly. From this example it can be seen, that the architecture is not modular on every layer, but more integral at lower layers. This case shows, that organizations do not necessarily modularize their system for internal openness to the same degree than for external openness, as re-modularizing a system also comes with a trade-off regarding costs and effort.

Thus, regarding the technical requirements for internal and for external openness, the results still hold in light of the cases, however, internal openness was not always strictly implemented in comparison to external openness. As the case of INCA showed, organizations do not necessarily design the system with the same degree of modularity in the case of internal openness. This may be due to a trade-off between costs and benefits, as designing the system in a more modular way could lead to additional expenses. However, in order to draw generalizable conclusions, a broader investigation would be necessary.

Implications of the case study results on network openness

In the second study, it was stated that firms pursue network openness to select the partners who supply complementary solutions for their ES. Network Openness has been rather seldom encountered in the cases. The infotainment platform case is an example which featured network openness, as they control which applications are allowed to run on their platform. In this case, this is partly motivated by safety and quality assurance aspects. Applications running on an infotainment system are more critical concerning these aspects than comparable applications which run for instance on as smart phone platform. To analyze the practical realization of network openness, additional cases would need to be elicited.

Implications of the case study results on market openness

Market Openness was the most common encountered form of organizational openness in the cases of the fourth study. The technical constraints and requirements found in the third study were to a large extent also found in the cases. Especially the need for modularizing the system in accordance with market openness has been emphasized in the cases. As previously discussed in the section "Implications of the case study results on internal openness", external openness creates additional need for modularization in the presence of safety or RT-constraints.

Table 17 shows, which kinds of organizational ES openness are implemented in the cases of the third study.

Table 17   Organizational forms of openness in cases

Case	Form of organizational ES openness
Raspberry PI	Market openness: Applications for the Raspberry PI can be implemented by any external users
Arduino	Market openness: Due to its open source respectively open hardware status, Arduino does not possess any restrictions regarding externals contributing to the platform
Google Glass	Market openness: Google Glass aims to build an ecosystem of external developers, a broad range of externals is the key towards reaching network effects
Project Ara	Market openness: Project Ara is yet in a beta stadium, but at the time of writing the aim is to spur a broad ecosystem of external innovators
SmartThings	Market openness: SmartThings constitutes an open platform whose success partly depends on the number of external firms integrating their ES with the SmartThings platform
Lego Mindstorms	Market openness: Lego Mindstorms is changed directly by the user, therefore implying market openness

INCA	Internal openness: INCA changes its platform on deeper layers depending on customer requirements in projects conducted by Fraunhofer; Market openness: Customers can develop and install additional applications on the platform
Prosyst E-Health	no data available as Prosyst sells the platform as a solution to platform providers
Infotainment System	Internal openness: The infotainment firm re-modularized their system to accelerate their own innovation cycles; Network openness: the infotainment platform provider decides which applications by external partners should be included in the platform
John Deere	Market openness: External companies can integrate trailers / implements and other agricultural equipment to the platform
Kuka Youbot	Market openness: Robotic platform can be extended by any users both on a HW as well as on the SW layer
Qivicon	Market openness: Qivicon relies on external firms to render the platform more attractive
RACE Project	*not yet defined*: The RACE platform has not yet been commercially implemented
Commercial vehicle platform	Internal openness: Firm internally opened its underlying ES for data-based applications
OpenXC	Market openness: Additional SW applications are supplied by externals
AutoPNP	Market openness: AutoPNP aims to allow externals to integrate their system with AutoPNP

The aim of the present part was to discuss the results of the empirical studies in light of their contribution to the individual and to the overall research question. It also reflected on the studies' approaches and its limitations. Regarding the overall research question, the primary limitation can be seen in the separate consideration of organizational and technical openness in two studies (third and fourth study). Although the cross-study discussion allowed taking a combined perspective, more detailed results could have been expected by a case study design which would have incorporated both perspectives. Other limitations of the individual studies can be seen partly in the applied method or in the sample size of the empirical data.

Furthermore, the second chapter of this part offered a cross-study discussion, which allowed to compare and improve the results of the individual studies.

Part V

Summary and Contribution

1 Summary

This thesis was concerned with exploring the phenomenon of open innovation in the context of embedded systems. It turned out, that the difference to 'conventional' OI is the requirement to open the underlying ES itself. Therefore, open innovation in ES goes beyond a mere opening of innovation processes, but has significant influence on the technical systems for which open innovation should be allowed.

In this summary chapter, I first of all want to summarize the overall structure of this thesis, and then reflect on the individual chapters and their contribution. The introduction was outlined in Part I. It was mainly concerned with presenting this thesis topic, its relevance and the specific need for exploring the phenomenon of OI in ES. Following in Part II, the foundations for this thesis have been presented. It introduced the core topics of this thesis, namely open innovation and embedded systems. To provide a theoretical perspective on the research topic, theory on openness, platforms and modularity has been introduced. Based on the foundations, Part III contained the empirical parts of this thesis. The results obtained in the third part have then been discussed in Part IV. In particular, this part compared and discussed the results of the single studies from an overall perspective towards its contribution to the research goal of this thesis. It also allowed a cross-validation between the different studies of this thesis. Table 18 presents the overview of this thesis from the introductory part in light of this thesis' results.

Table 18 Overview of the thesis

I.	**Introduction**
▪	Introduced the relevance of open innovation in embedded systems and this thesis' goals
▪	Presented the context of embedded systems and its need for distinct open innovation approaches
▪	Depicted the structure of the thesis and provided an overview of each part

II.	**Theoretical Foundations**
▪	Presented the topics of open innovation and embedded systems and elaborated the specific challenges of open innovation in embedded systems
▪	Introduced the theoretical perspectives of platform literature and modularity as a foundation for the later empirical analysis
▪	Outlined the research gap

III.	**Empirical Part**

- Presented the research design
- Study I: Explored three core OI processes in regards of the technical characteristics of ES
  - Conceptually explored and analyzed literature from the field of OI and ES
  - Showed the applicability and the constraints of the three core OI processes in the field of ES
- Study II: Operationalized organizational openness for OI in ES
  - Qualitative study based on 12 expert interviews
  - Presented three forms of organizational openness with corresponding organizational and technical constraints and requirements
- Study III: Operationalized technical openness and modularity of open ES
  - Comparative exploration of 16 case studies
  - Provided an operationalization of technical openness of ES
  - Presented modularization strategies for OI in ES
- Study IV: Explored open innovation without opening the embedded system
  - Qualitative exploration of 8 case vignettes
  - Identified two forms of OI without opening ES

IV.	**Discussion**

- Summarized the empirical research studies and their contribution towards the research question
- Provided a cross-study discussion to compare and validate the findings
- Reflected the research design used in this thesis

V.	**Summary and Contribution**

- Provides a summary of the thesis
- Presents the managerial and research implications of this thesis
- Shows future research possibilities

The next chapter will present the main findings of this thesis and present the managerial implications as well as the implications for research.

2   Contribution of this thesis

The following gives an overview of the thesis' research themes and its contributions:

To explore open innovation in ES, three main aspects had to be considered: First of all, the applicability of open innovation processes in ES has been analyzed. As a result, the challenges and constraints of the three core OI processes as outlined by Gassmann & Enkel (2004) have been studied. This first study showed, that opening ES for open innovation is especially influenced by technical characteristics of ES such as *safety* aspects and *RT constraints*. The results of this study provided the base upon which the other two empirical studies are built on.

The second study dealt with the required organizational opening of ES firms to enable open innovation. For this study, 12 expert interviews have been conducted. Here, it was found, that especially the technical characteristics of ES as well as organizational requirements such as the protection of IP as well as liability have a large influence to whom and to what degree an ES can be opened. These factors led to three different forms of organizational openness: *internal openness, network openness* and *market openness*. Internal openness was also seen as a prerequisite for the two *'external'* forms of openness, namely *network and market openness*. Furthermore, a detailed overview of each of the factors influencing firm's organizational openness decision has been provided.

The third study tackled the technical openness required for conducting open innovation in the context of ES. As a data source for this study, I relied on case studies from a broad variety of different industries. As a result, the notion of openness in ES was operationalized which allows an in-depth understanding of the requirements of open innovation in ES. Several forms of openness have been encountered in the cases: *data openness, application openness, operating system openness and hardware openness*. Furthermore, another key result was the exploration of design aspects of ES for open innovation. In particular, it was shown how ES can be modularized to allow open innovation. Thus, it extended research in open innovation by exploring how OI influences the design of an underlying technical system.

An overview of the results of this thesis is given in Table 19.

Table 19   Results of the thesis

Study 1	The study analyzed the implications of the technical characteristics on the three core OI processes
	The Outside-In process is especially applicable for OI in ES
	Presented the constraints and challenges of OI in ES due to the characteristics of ES
	Provides guidance for the implementation of OI processes for ES
Study 2	The study presents different forms of organizationally opening ES: internal openness, as well as the two forms of external openness (network and market openness)
	Internal openness has the same technical requirements than the two forms of external openness
	Study offers the technical and organizational factors which influence the selection of the organizational opening of ES for OI
	Firms can choose different forms of organizational openness according to the technical risks but also according to business objectives like IP protection etc.

Study 3	The study presents the technical forms of opening ES for OI: data openness, application openness, operating system openness and hardware openness
	For each of the discovered forms of openness, potential modularizations are presented
	The discovered ways of modularizing ES tackle the technical challenges of ES like safety, security and RT-constraints
	Study provides guidelines for firms to open and design their systems in accordance with OI
Study 4	In the study, two types of OI without opening the ES were found: OI by hacking and OI through the creation of new interfaces
	OI without opening more likely for ES which are not subject to ES characteristics like safety or RT constraints
	Technically, the system already needs to have a sufficient degree of general-purpose characteristics
	Firms can incorporate unforeseen OI initiatives by devising an openness strategy

2.1   Managerial implications

This thesis aimed to explore how embedded systems can be opened for open innovation. The decision to open an embedded system is of relevance to both a management as well as a technical audience. It has far-reaching implications not only regarding the design of the ES, but also towards the business model pursued by an ES firm. Furthermore, it requires knowledge both of the technical as well as the organizational challenges and risks. Regarding the managerial audience, one target group of this thesis are decision makers defining the strategy of a firm and its products. Furthermore, it would involve both product managers as well as innovation managers. Regarding the technical audience, the thesis' results are relevant for system architects but also for technical project managers.

2.1.1   Implications for decision makers

In many companies selling 'traditional' ES, *managers* view the decisions regarding the ES parts of their products mainly under a costs and efficiency perspective. Therefore, the move towards open innovation represents a fundamental change regarding future sources of innovation. A key decision managers need to take when implementing open innovation is to determine a particular *degree of openness*, which corresponds with their strategic goals. This decision is dependent on what parts of their ES constitute *core* parts whose intellectual property needs to be protected. Associated with the question of the *degree of openness* is the level of control firms can retain while opening their system.

The degree of openness has both a technical as well as an organizational facet. For decision makers in management, especially the organizational side of openness has to be determined. The third empirical study of this thesis identified three different types of organizational openness, which are depicted in Figure 16.

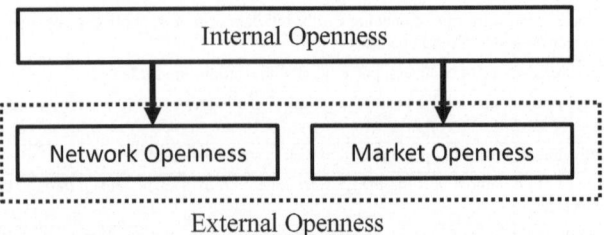

Figure 16 Organizational forms of openness in ES

Primarily, firms have to choose between internal and external openness. Although internal openness does not enable open innovation, it helps the ES firm to become much more flexible concerning future adaptations of their system. Furthermore, implementing external openness at a later stage is also facilitated by internal openness. To implement external openness, firms can choose between two approaches. By pursuing network openness, firms would self-select potential contributors, whom it would be allowed to enhance the system. This approach goes beyond a classical purchaser-contractor relationship, as the contractors would not merely develop extensions according to the specifications of the purchaser, but would have the possibility to contribute their own ideas. Such an approach would make sense for various reasons: First of all, it allows to retain more control over the development of the platform, and thus being better able to appropriate returns from sales. Secondly, firms could keep unwanted external actors or competitors away from the ES platform. In addition, network openness is appropriate for systems which are more critical concerning safety aspects of have certain certification requirements. For instance, for ES platforms in the healthcare or in the automotive sector, the system's function need to be certified before they can be released on the market.

In contrast, when the ES firms' aim is to build an *ecosystem* around their system, they would pursue market openness. With this form of openness, the number of potential contributors would not be constrained by the ES provider. However, decision makers would also have to deal with different risks in the case of market openness. One aspect ES firms have to consider is the implementation of quality assurance processes. As market openness does not put constraints on who is contributing to the system, this may result in additions which are of lower quality of not properly tested. Managers can chose between different levels of control. For the sake of comparison, different approaches can for instance be found in the smart phone domain, with the Apple iOS and the Google Android ecosystems. Apple as the provider of the iOS platform for instance has rather strict requirements regarding quality assurance when deploying apps for their platform. In contrast, the Android ecosystem leaves more freedom for externals but which also entails additional risks. The perspective of how to organize an ecosystem for ES also constitutes a limitation of this thesis, which could be tackled by future research.

2.1.2 Implications for system architects

The decision to open an ES is usually taken by the management. However, the technical design decisions are mainly taken by technical staff, e.g. by system architects. On a technical level, the results brought forward four different technical forms of ES openness (Figure 17) and the modularization requirements for each of these forms of openness. These technical forms of openness correspond with the decision by managers regarding the *degree of openness*. Thus, they represent the technical implementation of the firm's decision to pursue open innovation. Each of the technical forms of openness is associated to a particular layer in the layer model of embedded systems. System architects could open each of these layers in order to direct open innovation at specific parts of the system. This can take place at the data layer, the application layer, the operating system layer or at the hardware layer.

Whereas openness at the data layer is relatively easy to implement, openness at lower levels requires more efforts regarding the modular design of the system. Especially for application openness, system architects need to take the typical requirements in terms of safety, RT etc. into account. In order to effectively handle these requirements, partitioning and separation are key principles system architects need to consider. For system architects, implementing hardware openness does not amount to the same effort. Basically, the effort mainly results from providing externals standardizes interfaces allowing them to connect additional hardware modules. In addition, ES firms must provide means for externals to integrate hardware modules on the software layer.

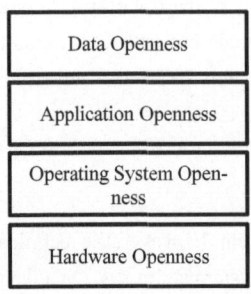

Data Openness	• Outsourcing of third-party applications to external devices • Data access via abstraction layer: e.g. proxy module or separate bus system
Application Openness	• Partitioning of execution environment for additional applications • Separation of bus systems to guarantee non-interference with critical system's functions
Operating System Openness	• provide limited access to OS, e.g. by sandbox approach
Hardware Openness	• Support for a broad variety of different standards • Abstraction from different connectivity standards and hardware details

Figure 17 Technical forms of openness in ES

A further aspect resulting from the involvement of externals is the need to manage the evolving community respectively the ecosystem around the platforms. The additional effort has already been emphasized by the notion of organizational openness. This requires additional management skills that go beyond technical competences.

Furthermore, companies have to provide additional support and documentation. Further implications of implementing openness can also be seen in need for additional experts respectively know-how. In contrast to 'simpler' ES, which were designated for a particular purpose, ES which are opened have to fulfill a broader range of use cases. This in turn also increases the overall complexity of the system.

2.2   Research implications

This thesis brought forward the topic of open innovation in embedded systems. This extends both the body of knowledge in open innovation as well as in embedded systems. The contribution to research in open innovation lies in the extension of open innovation processes in the domain of embedded systems. The technical aspects of embedded systems generate a wider set of challenges and constraints not encountered in non-technical settings. Although embedded systems possess idiosyncratic characteristics, it exemplifies the process of applying open innovation in a technical domain. From this research follows that open innovation in ES needs to be addressed more holistically, as the technical aspects of ES influence potential ES processes. At the same time, a further contribution was the results regarding the influence of open innovation on the technical artefact, namely ES.

As this thesis sets the foundations for exploring open innovation in ES, there is still a range of research topics, which need to be addressed. On the one hand, the studies conducted for this thesis have certain limitations that need to be addressed. Table 20 shows additional research resulting from this thesis' studies. These topics would provide further details regarding the topics considered in this thesis.

Table 20   Further research need building on this thesis

Topic	Exemplary research questions
Challenges for OI in ES	What additional industry-related challenges and constraints for OI do ES firms need to consider? How can they be tackled?
Organizational design for OI in ES	How can the organizational forms of openness be realized? - Elicit cases for each form of openness What is the impact of liability issues on openness? - Measures to reduce liability for ES firms Which organizational support do external innovators need? How can firms manage the ecosystem around open ES?
Openness of ES	How can ES be opened in a cost-effective way? What role do specific openness measures, e.g. open hardware play for open innovation? What role do other measures play for the openness of ES, such as documentation and support?
Design of ES for open innovation	How can ES providers ensure the security of open ES? - Implementation of adequate security mechanisms What design measures can be employed to facilitate external development?

On the other hand, there is also further research outside the boundaries of this thesis. The following table gives an overview of related aspects of OI in ES, which were not part of the research goals of this thesis, but would nevertheless provide additional insights into surrounding aspects.

Table 21   Further research need outside this thesis' scope

Topic	Exemplary research questions
Inside-Out process in ES	How can ES firms still control their systems when pursuing the Inside-Out process? What are the technical and organizational requirements for the Inside-Out process in ES?
Community management for open ES	How can ES firms support external users for open innovation? How can ES firms manage the ecosystem to spur OI in ES?
Business models for open ES	What influence does opening of ES have on existing business models (of the ES providers)? How can business models for open ES be categorized?

Regarding open innovation, this thesis focuses on the 'outside-in' process, thereby neglecting the other direction of open innovation, namely the 'inside-out' process. Opening an ES also makes sense for the inside-out process, for instance, when an ES firm has a variety of ideas but not the necessary resources to implement them. The underlying need for opening the system could be similar for such scenarios, however, it would need further investigation.

The topic of community management would also be worthwhile to explore in the context of ES. Obviously, external innovators may need (tool) support or documentation. However, community management could also help to realize other goals: questions, which would be of interest, are for instance, how ES firms can spark innovation by externals by a proper management of the community. Another aspect would be how community management can help the company to shape the trajectory of an ES platform.

Further research should also address the business side of open innovation in ES. The changes due to openness of ES also have profound implications on the business models. The opening of an ES for OI results in significant changes for both a firms' value creation as well as its value appropriation strategy. Due to the broad variety of different ES, the consideration of business models also needs to incorporate an industry-specific focus.

References

Abdelkafi, N., Blecker, T. and Raasch, C. 2009. "From Open Source in the Digital to the Physical World: A Smooth Transfer?" *Management Decision* 47(10): 1610–32.

Aguiar, A., and Hessel, F. 2010. "Embedded Systems' Virtualization: The next Challenge?" *Rapid System Prototyping (RSP), 2010.*

Alexandrov, A., Ibel, M., Schauser, K., and Scheiman, C. 1997. "Extending the Operating System at the User-Level: The Ufo Global File System." In *USENIX Annual Technical Conference*: 77–90.

Alspaugh, T., Hazeline U., and Scacchi, W. 2009. "Analyzing Software Licenses in Open Architecture Software Systems." *2009 ICSE Workshop on Emerging Trends in Free/Libre/Open Source Software Research and Development*: 54–57.

Anvaari, M, and Jansen, S. 2010. "Evaluating Architectural Openness in Mobile Software Platforms." In *4th European Conference of Software Architecture*, , 85–92.

Armstrong, C. E., and Shimizu, K. 2007. "A Review of Approaches to Empirical Research on the Resource-Based View of the Firm ." *Journal of Management* 33(6): 959–86.

Baldwin, C. 2012. "Organization Design for Distributed Innovation." *Harvard Business School Finance Working Paper.*

Baldwin, C, and Clark, K. 2004. "Modularity in the Design of Complex Engineering Systems." *Complex Engineered Systems Understanding Complex Systems* (January): 175–205.

Baldwin, C, and Henkel, J. 2011. "The Impact of Modularity on Intellectual Property and Value Appropriation." *Harvard Business School Finance Working Paper.*

Baldwin, C, and von Hippel, E. 2011. "Modeling a Paradigm Shift: From Producer Innovation to User and Open Collaborative Innovation." *Organization Science* 22(6): 1399–1417.

Balka, K, Raasch, C. and Herstatt, C. 2009. "Open Source beyond Software : An Empirical Investigation of the Open Design Phenomenon." *R&D Management Conference* (April): 1–28.

Barney, J. 1991. "Firm Resources and Sustained Competitive Advantage." *Journal of Management* 17(1): 99–120.

Barney, J. 1995. "Looking inside for Competitive Advantage." *The Academy of Management Executive (1993-2005)* 9(4): 49–61.

Basole, R, and Karla, J. 2011. "On the Evolution of Mobile Platform Ecosystem Structure and Strategy." *Business & Information Systems Engineering* 3(5): 313–22.

Von Bertalanffy, L. 1950. "The Theory of Open Systems in Physics and Biology." *Science (New York, N.Y.)* 111(2872): 23–29.

Von Bertalanffy, L. 1968. *General System Theory.* New York, NY: George Braziller Inc.

Bogers, M, and West, J. 2012. "Managing Distributed Innovation: Strategic Utilization of Open and User Innovation." *Creativity and Innovation Management* 21(1): 61–75.

Booch, G. 1994. *Object-Oriented Analysis and Design.* Reading, MA: Addison-Wesley.

Bosch, J. 2009. "From Software Product Lines to Software Ecosystems." In *Proceedings of the 13th International Software Product Line Conference*, 111–19.

Boudreau, K. 2008. "Opening the Platform vs. Opening the Complementary Good? The Effect on Product Innovation in Handheld Computing." *HEC working paper.*

Boudreau, K. 2010. "Open Platform Strategies and Innovation: Granting Access vs. Devolving Control." *Management Science* 56(10): 1849–72.

Boudreau, K. 2011. "Let a Thousand Flowers Bloom? An Early Look at Large Numbers of Software App Developers and Patterns of Innovation." *Organization Science*: 1–19.

Brown, I. 2013. "Entre Firme et Usagers : Des Biens Génératifs D ' Usages Théorie Des Biens Comme Espaces de Conception." Mines ParisTech.

Broy, M. 2006. "Challenges in Automotive Software Engineering." *Proceeding of the 28th international conference on Software engineering - ICSE '06*: 33.

Brusoni, S, and Prencipe, A. 2001. "Unpacking the Black Box of Modularity: Technologies, Products and Organizations." *Industrial and Corporate Change*: 179–205.

Brusoni, S, and Prencipe, A. 2006. "Making Design Rules: A Multidomain Perspective." *Organization Science* 17(2): 179–89.

Buckley, J, Mens, T., Zenger, M., Rashid, A. and Kniesel, G. 2005. "Towards a Taxonomy of Software Change." *Journal of Software Maintenance and Evolution: Research and Practice* 17(5): 309–32.

Burkard, C., Widjaja, T. and Buxmann, P.. 2012. "Software Ecosystems." *Business & Information Systems Engineering* 4(1): 41–44.

Cabigiosu, A., Zirpoli, F. and Camuffo, A. 2012. "Modularity, Interfaces Definition and the Integration of External Sources of Innovation in the Automotive Industry." *Research Policy*.

Campagnolo, D, and Camuffo, A.. 2009. "The Concept of Modularity in Management Studies: A Literature Review." *International Journal of Management Reviews*.

Chen, K., and Liu, R. 2005. "Interface Strategies in Modular Product Innovation." *Technovation* 25(7): 771–82.

Chesbrough, H W. 2003. Harvard Business Publishing *The New Imperative for Creating and Profiting from Technology*. Boston, MA: Harvard Business School Press.

Chesbrough, H.W. 2006. In H. Chesbrough, W. Vanhaverbeke, and J. West (eds.), Open Innovation: Researching A New Paradigm *Open Innovation: A New Paradigm for Understanding Industrial Innovation*. Oxford: Oxford University Press.

Chesbrough, H.W, and Crowther, A. 2006. "Beyond High Tech: Early Adopters of Open Innovation in Other Industries." *R & D Management* 36(3): 229–36.

Clark, K.B., and Baldwin, C. 2000. 1 *Design Rules: The Power of Modularity.*"Malden, MA: Blackwell.

Coffey, A, and Atkinson, P. 1996. *Making Sense of Qualitative Data: Complementary Research Strategies*. Thousand Oaks: SAGE Publications.

Cohen, WM, and Levinthal, DA. 1990. "Absorptive Capacity: A New Perspective on Learning and Innovation." *Administrative science quarterly* 35(1): 128–52.

Colfer, L, and Baldwin, C. 2010. "The Mirroring Hypothesis : Theory , Evidence and Exceptions Lyra Colfer The Mirroring Hypothesis : Theory , Evidence and Exceptions." *Harvard Business School Working Paper* No. 10-058.

Creswell, J.W. 1994. *Research Design: Qualitative, Quantitative, and Mixed Methods Approaches*. Thousand Oaks, CA: Sage.

Dedrick, J., and West, J. 2003. "Why Firms Adopt Open Source Platforms: A Grounded Theory of Innovation and Standards Adoption." *MISQ Special Issue Workshop - -Standard Making: A Critical Research Frontier for Informations Systems*: 236–57.

Drechsler, W, and Natter, M. 2012. "Understanding a Firm's Openness Decisions in Innovation." *Journal of Business Research* 65(3): 438–45.

Ebert, C., and Jones, C. 2009. "Embedded Software: Facts, Figures, and Future." *Computer* 42(4): 42–52.

Eisenhardt, K. M. 1989. "Building Theories from Case Study Research." *The Academy of Management Review* 14(4): 532.

Eisenhardt, K. M., and Graebner, M. E.. 2007. "Theory Building From Cases: Opportunities and Challenges." *Academy of Management Journal* 50(1): 25–32.

Eisenmann, T, Parker, G. Van Alstyne, M. 2008. "Opening Platforms : How , When and Why ?" *Harvard Business Review*.

Eklund, U., and Bosch, J. 2012. "Using Architecture for Multiple Levels of Access to an Ecosystem Platform." *Proceedings of the 8th international ACM SIGSOFT conference on Quality of Software Architectures - QoSA '12*: 143.

Elmquist, M., Fredberg, T., and Ollila, S. 2009. "Exploring the Field of Open Innovation." *European Journal of Innovation Management* 12(3): 326–45.

Ethiraj, S. K., Levinthal, D. and Roy, R. R.. 2008. "The Dual Role of Modularity: Innovation and Imitation." *Management Science* 54(5): 939–55.

Ethiraj, S. and Levinthal, D. 2004. "Modularity and Innovatiuon in Complex Systems." *Management Science* 50(2): 159–73.

Eysenbach, G. 2001. "What Is E-Health?" *Journal of medical Internet research* 3(2): E20.

Feller, J, and Fitzgerald, B. 2002. *Understanding Open Source Software Development*. Addison-Wesley Professional; 1 edition.

Fernandes, J., Lamb, L., Machado, R. and Wagner, F. 2009. "Recent Advances in Model-Based Methodologies for Pervasive and Embedded Software." *ACM SIGSOFT Software Engineering Notes* 34(5): 37–39.

Fine, C., Golany, B., and Naseraldin, H. 2005. "Modeling Tradeoffs in Three-Dimensional Concurrent Engineering: A Goal Programming Approach." *Journal of Operations Management* 23(3-4): 389–403.

Fixson, SK. 2001. "Three Perspectives on Modularity - a Literature Review of a Product Concept for Assembled Hardware Products." *Working Paper Series* (October).

Fortiss. 2011. "Mehr Software (im) Wagen : Informations- Und Kommunikations- Technik (IKT) Als Motor Der Elektro Mobilität Der Zukunft." *eCar-IKT-Systemarchitektur für Elektromobilität* (im).

Fosfuri, A., Giarratana, M. S., and Luzzi, A. 2008. "The Penguin Has Entered the Building: The Commercialization of Open Source Software Products." *Organization Science* 19(2): 292–305.

Funk, J. 2008. "Systems, Components and Modular Design: The Case of the US Semiconductor Industry." *International Journal of Technology Management* 42(4): 387–413.

Galvin, P. 2008. "A Case Study of Knowledge Protection and Diffusion for Innovation: Managing Knowledge in the Mobile Telephone Industry." *International Journal of Technology Management* 42(4): 426–38.

Gärtner, A. 2010. "MDD 2007/47/EG: Software Als Medizinprodukt." *E-Health.com*: 1–20.

Garud, R, and Kumaraswamy, A. 1993. "Changing Competitive Dynamics in Network Industries: An Exploration of Sun Microsystems' Open Systems Strategy." *Strategic Management Journal* 14: 351–69.

Gassmann, O, and Enkel, E. 2004. "Towards a Theory of Open Innovation: Three Core Process Archetypes." *R&D management conference*: 1–18.

Gawer, A. 2009. "Platform Dynamics and Strategies: From Products to Services." *Platforms, markets and innovation*: 45–76.

Gawer, A, and Cusumano, M. 2002. *Platform Leadership: How Intel, Microsoft, and Cisco Drive Industry Innovation.* Harvard Business Review Press.

Giannopoulou, E., Yström, A., and Ollila, S. 2011. "Turning Open Innovation Into Practice: Open Innovation Research Through the Lens of Managers." *International Journal of Innovation Management* 15(03): 505–24.

Graaf, B., Lormans, M. and Toetenel, H. 2003. "Embedded Software Engineering: The State of the Practice." *Software, IEEE* 20(6): 61–69.

Grøtnes, E. 2009. "Standardization as Open Innovation: Two Cases from the Mobile Industry." *Information Technology & People* 22(4): 367–81.

Gruber, M., and Henkel, J. 2006. "New Ventures Based on Open Innovation an Empirical Analysis of Start-up Firms in Embedded Linux." *International Journal of Technology Management* 33(4): 356–72.

Grunberg, E. 1978. "'Complexity' and 'Open Systems' in Economic Discourse." *Journal of Economic Issues* 12(3): 541–60.

Gunter, C, and Alur, R.. 2003. "Open APIs for Embedded Systems : A Challenge for the Science of Design." *Lecture Notes in Computer Science* 2743(October): 225–47.

Halsall, F.. 1996. *Data Communications, Computer Networks and Open Systems*. 4th ed. Addison-Wesley.

Hansen, A, and Howard, TJ. 2013. "The Current State of Open Source Hardware: The Need for an Open Source Development Platform" eds. Amaresh Chakrabarti and Raghu V. Prakash. *ICoRD'13*.

Haruvy, E., Sethi, S. and Zhou, J. 2008. "Open Source Development with a Commercial Complementary Product or Service." *Production and Operations Management* 17(1): 29–43.

Heath, S. 2002. Newnes *Embedded Systems Design*. 2nd Editio. Oxford: Newnes.

Heiser, G. 2008. "The Role of Virtualization in Embedded Systems." *Proceedings of the 1st workshop on Isolation and integration in embedded systems - IIES '08*: 11–16.

Henkel, J. 2006. "Selective Revealing in Open Innovation Processes: The Case of Embedded Linux." *Research Policy* 35(7): 953–69.

Henkel, J., and Baldwin, C. 2010. "Modularity for Value Appropriation –How to Draw the Boundaries of Intellectual Property." *Harvard Business School Finance Working Paper* (11-054): 46.

Henkel, J., Baldwin, C., and Shih, W. 2012. "IP Modularity: Profiting from Innovation by Aligning Product Architecture with Intellectual Property." *Harvard Business School Finance Working Paper*.

Henzinger, T., and Sifakis, J. 2007. "The Discipline of Embedded Systems Design." *Computer* 40(10): 32–40.

Hilkert, D., Benlian, A., and Hess, T. 2011. "The Openness of Smartphone Software Platforms–A Framework and Preliminary Empirical Findings from the Developers' Perspective." *41. Annual Conference of the Gesellschaft für Informatik (INFORMATIK 2011). Springer (Lecture Notes in Informatics), Berlin, German y*: 192.

Hinterhuber, A. 2002. "Value Chain Orchestration in Action and the Case of the Global Agrochemical Industry." *Long Range Planning* 35(6): 615–35.

von Hippel, E. 1986. "Lead Users: A Source of Novel Product Concepts." *Management Science* 32(7): 791–805.

Von Hippel, E. 2006. *Democratizing Innovation*. Cambridge, MA: MIT Press.

von Hippel, E, and von Krogh, G. 2006. "Free Revealing and the Private-Collective Model for Innovation Incentives." *R and D Management* 36(3): 295–306.

Huff, A.S., Möslein, K.M. and Reichwald, R. 2013. *Leading Open Innovation*. Cambridge, MA.: MIT Press.

Jansen, S., Brinkkemper, S., Hunink, I., and Demir, C. 2008. "Pragmatic and Opportunistic Reuse in Innovative Start-up Companies." *IEEE Software* 25(6): 42–49.

Johannessen, P., Törner, F. and Torin, J. 2004. "Actuator Based Hazard Analysis for Safety Critical Systems." *Computer Safety, Reliability, and Security* 3219: 130–41.

King, N. 1998. "Template Analysis." In *Qualitative Methods and Analysis in Organizational Research*, Thousand Oaks: Sage.

King, N, and C Horrocks. 2010. *Interviews in Qualitative Research*. SAGE Publications Ltd.

Klatt, B., and Krogmann, K. 2008. "Software Extension Mechanisms." *Fakultät für Informatik, Karlsruhe, Germany, Interner Bericht*.

Langlois, R., and Garzarelli, G. 2008. "Of Hackers and Hairdressers: Modularity and the Organizational Economics of Open-source Collaboration." In *Industry & Innovation*, , 125–43.

Langlois, R. 2002. "Modularity in Technology and Organization." *Journal of Economic Behavior & Organization* 49(1): 19–37.

Laursen, K., and Salter, A. 2006. "Open for Innovation: The Role of Openness in Explaining Innovation Performance Among U.K. Manufacturing Firms." *Strategic Management Journal* 27(2): 131–50.

Lecocq, X, and Demil, B. 2006. "Strategizing Industry Structure: The Case of Open Systems in a Low-Tech Industry." *Strategic Management Journal* 27(9): 891–98.

Lee, E., Seshia, S. 2015. LeeSeshia.org *Introduction to Embedded Systems: A Cyber-Physical Systems Approach*. Lulu.com.

Liggesmeyer, P., and Trapp, M. 2009. "Trends in Embedded Software Engineering." *Software, IEEE* 26(3): 19–25.

Loasby, B. 2003. "Closed Models and Open Systems." *Journal of Economic Methodology* 10(3): 285–306.

MacCormack, A., Baldwin, C. and Rusnak, J. 2012. "Exploring the Duality between Product and Organizational Architectures: A Test of the 'Mirroring' Hypothesis." *Research Policy* 41(8): 1309–24.

MacCormack, A., Baldwin, C., and Rusnak, J. 2010. "The Architecture of Complex Systems: Do 'Core-Periphery' Structures Dominate?" In *Academy of Management Proceedings*,

Marwedel, P. 2011. *Embedded System Design - Embedded Systems Foundations of Cyber-Phisical Systems*. Secaucus, NJ: Springer.

Mayring, P. 2002. *Einführung in Die Qualitative Sozialforschung: Eine Anleitung Zu Qualitativem Denken*. Beltz.

Mellis, D., and Buechley, L. 2012. "Collaboration in Open-Source Hardware: Third-Party Variations on the Arduino Duemilanove." : 1175–78.

Mikkola, J.H. 2003. "Modularity, Component Outsourcing, and Inter-Firm Learning." *R & D Management* 33(4): 439–54.

Mikkola, J.H. 2006. "Capturing the Degree of Modularity Embedded in Product Architectures*." *Journal of Product Innovation Management* 23(2): 128–46.

Mikkola, J.H., and Skjøtt-Larsen, T. 2006. "Platform Management: Implication for New Product Development and Supply Chain Management." *European Business Review* 18(3): 214–30.

Miles, M., Huberman, M., and Saldana, J. 2013. *Qualitative Data Analysis: An Methods Sourcebook*. 2nd ed. SAGE Publications, Inc.

Newey, L. 2010. "Wearing Different Hats: How Absorptive Capacity Differs in Open Innovation." *International Journal of Innovation Management* 14(04): 703–31.

Noergaard, T. 2005. *Embedded Systems Architecture: A Comprehensive Guide for Engineers and Programmers.* Newnes.

Parker, G., and Van Alstyne, M. 2005. "Two-Sided Network Effects: A Theory of Information Product Design." *Management Science* 51(10): 1494–1504.

Parker, G., Van Alstyne, M. 2010. "Innovation, Openness & Platform Control." *Proceedings of the 11th ACM conference on Electronic commerce - EC '10* 4684-08: 95.

Parnas, D. L. 1972. "On the Criteria to Be Used in Decomposing Systems into Modules." *Communications of the ACM* 15(12): 1053–58.

Pimentel, A., Erbas, C., and Polstra, S. 2006. "A Systematic Approach to Exploring Embedded System Architectures at Multiple Abstraction Levels." *IEEE Transactions on Computers* 55(2): 99–112.

Pimmler, T., and Eppinger, S. 1994. "Integration Analysis of Product Decompositions." *ASME Design Theory and Methodology Conference (Minneapolis)* 68(September): 343–51.

Pondy, L., and Mitroff, I. 1979. "Beyond Open System Models of Organization." *Research in organizational behavior:* 119–38.

Raasch, C., and Herstatt, C. 2011. "How Companies Capture Value from Open Design." *International Journal of Information and Decision Sciences* 3(1): 39.

Raasch, C., Herstatt, C, and Balka, K. 2009. "On the Open Design of Tangible Goods." *R&D Management* 39(4): 382–93.

Rashid, R., Baron, R., Forin, A, Golub, D., Jones, M., Julin, D. Orr, D. and Sanzi, R. 1989. "Mach: A Foundation for Open Systems." In *In Proceedings of the 2nd Workshop on Workstation Operating Systems. IEEE, September,*

Raymond, E. 1999. "The Cathedral and the Bazaar." *Knowledge, Technology & Policy* 12(3): 23–49.

Reichwald, R, and Piller, F. 2005. "Open Innovation : Kunden Als Partner Im Innovationsprozess" eds. Walter Habenicht, Stefan Foschiani, and Gerhard Wäscher.

Reichwald, R, and Piller, F. 2006. *Interaktive Wertschöpftung: Open Innovation, Individualisierung Und Neue Formen Der Arbeitsteilung.* Boston: Harvard Business School Press.

Saglietti, F. 2004. "Licensing Reliable Embedded Software for Safety-Critical Applications." *Real-Time Systems* 28(2/3): 217–36.

Saltzer, J.H., and Kaashoek, M.F. 2009. *Principles of Computer System Design: An Introduction.* Morgan Kaufmann.

Sanchez, R, and Collins, R. 2001. "Competing—and Learning—in Modular Markets." *Long Range Planning* 34(6): 645–67.

Sanchez, R, and Mahoney, J. 1996. "Modularity, Flexibility and Knowledge Management in Product and Organization Design." *Strategic Management Journal* 17(Special Issue: Knowledge and the firm (Winter, 1996)): 63–76.

Sangiovanni-Vincentelli, A., and Di Natale, M. 2007. "Embedded System Design for Automotive Applications." *Computer* 40(10): 42–51.

Schilling, M.A.. 2000. "Toward a General Modular Systems Theory and Its Application to Interfirm Product Modularity." *Academy of management review* 25(2): 312–34.

Schlagwein, D., Schoder, D., and Fischbach, K. 2010. "Openness of Information Resources–A Framework-Based Comparison of Mobile Platforms." *Information Systems.*

Shapiro, C., and Varian, H. 1999. *Information Rules: A Strategic Guide to the Network Economy*. Boston, MA: Harvard Business School Press.

Simcoe, T. 2006. "Open Standards and Intellectual Property Rights." In *Open Innovation: Researching a New Paradigm*, Oxford University Press, 161–83.

Simon, H.A. 1962. "The Architecture of Complexity." *Proceedings of the american philosophical society* 106(6): 467–82.

Soeldner, C., Roth, A., Danzinger, F. and Moeslein, K. 2013. "Towards Open Innovation in Embedded Systems." *Proceedings of the Nineteenth Americas Conference on Information Systems* (1): 1–8.

Soeldner, C., Roth, A. and Moeslein, K. 2015. "Opening Embedded Systems for Open Innovation." *Pacific Asia Conference on Information Systems (PACIS 2015), Singapore*.

Soeldner, C., Danzinger, F., Roth, A., and Moeslein, K. 2012. "Open Innovation by Opening Embedded Systems." *Gemeinschaften in Neuen Medien (GeNeMe '12)*: 33–46.

Spaanenburg, L., and Spaanenburg, H. 2011. *Cloud Connectivity and Embedded Sensory Systems*. Springer.

Teece, D. 1986. "Profiting from Technological Innovation: Implications for Integration, Collaboration, Licensing and Public Policy." *Research policy* 15(February): 285–305.

Tushman, M., and Murmann, J. 1998. "Dominant Designs, Technology Cycles, and Organizational Outcomes." *Research in Organizational Behavior* 20: 231–66.

Ulrich, K. 1995. "The Role of Product Architecture in the Manufacturing Firm." *Research Policy* 24(3): 419–40.

Ulrich, K, and Eppinger, S. 2000. *Product Design and Development*. New York: McGraw-Hill.

Vallance, R., Kiani, S., and Nayfeh, S. 2001. "Open Design of Manufacturing Equipment." *Proceedings of the CHIRP 1st International Conference on Agile, Reconfigurable Manufacturing*: 1–12.

Volberda, H., Foss, N., and Lyles, M. 2010. "Absorbing the Concept of Absorptive Capacity: How to Realize Its Potential in the Organization Field." *Organization Science* 21(4): 931–51.

Vonkrogh, G, and Spaeth, S. 2007. "The Open Source Software Phenomenon: Characteristics That Promote Research☆." *The Journal of Strategic Information Systems* 16(3): 236–53.

Wade, M., and Hulland, J. 2004. "Review: The Resource-Based View and Information Systems Research: Review, Extension, and Suggestions for Future Research." *MIS quarterly* 28(1): 107–42.

Wallace, M., and Richardson, S. 2012. "Getting Started with Raspberry Pi." : 175.

Wartena, F., Muskens, J, and Schmitt, L. 2009. "Continua: The Impact of a Personal Telehealth Ecosystem." *2009 International Conference on eHealth, Telemedicine, and Social Medicine*: 13–18.

Webster, J, and Watson, R. 2002. "Analyzing the Past to Prepare for the Future: Writing a Literature Review." *Management Information Systems Quarterly* 26(2).

Weick, K.E. 1976. "Educational Organizations as Loosely Coupled Systems." *Administrative Science Quarterly* 21(1): 1–19.

Wernerfelt, B. 1984. "A Resource Based View of the Firm." *Health marketing quarterly* 25(4): 361–82.

West, J. 2003. "How Open Is Open Enough? Melding Proprietary and Open Source Platform Strategies." *Research Policy* 32(7): 1259–85.

West, J., and Dedrick, J. 2000. "Innovation and Control in Standards Architectures: The Rise and Fall of Japan's PC-98." *Information Systems Research* 11(2): 197–216.

West, J. and Gallagher, S. 2006a. "Challenges of Open Innovation: The Paradox of Firm Investment in Open source Software." *R&D Management* 36(3): 319–31.

West, J., and Gallagher, S. 2006b. Open innovation researching a new paradigm *Patterns of Open Innovation in Open Source Software*. eds. H. Chesbrough, W. Vanhaverbeke, and J. West. Oxford University Press.

West, J., and O'Mahony, S. 2008. "The Role of Participation Architecture in Growing Sponsored Open Source Communities." *Industry & Innovation* 15(2): 145–68.

West, J., Vanhaverbeke, W. and Chesbrough, H. 2006. "Open Innovation: A Research Agenda." In *Open Innovation: Researching a New Paradigm*, eds. HW Chesbrough, W Vanhaverbeke, and J West. Oxford: Oxford University Press, 285–307.

Wolf, W. H. 2001. Design Automation for Embedded Systems *Computers as Components: Principles of Embedded Computing System Design*. Morgan Kaufmann.

Yin, R.K. 2008. *Case Study Research: Design and Methods*. Thousand Oaks, CA: Sage Publications, Inc.

Ziegler, S., and Müller, A. 2008. BITKOM *Studie Zur Bedeutung Des Sektors Embedded-Systeme in Deutschland*. Berlin, Germany: BITKOM.

Annexes

Annex A   Complete list of internet sources used in study 3

The cases in study 3 (Part III, 4) were to a considerable degree based on internet sources. To allow the readers to get more details about the data retrieved for each case, the table below provides a complete list on which internet sources the cases were based on.

Table 22   Internet sources used in study 3

Case	Sources
Raspberry PI	https://www.raspberrypi.org/help/faqs/#introWhatIs http://www.raspberrypi.org/raspberry-pi-compute-module-new-product/ https://www.raspberrypi.org/help/faqs/#generalSoCUsed http://www.raspberrypi.org/raspberry-pi-compute-module-new-product/ http://makezine.com/2014/04/07/new-raspberry-pi-compute-module-unveiled/
Arduino	http://arduino.cc/en/Guide/Introduction http://arduino.cc/en/Main/FAQ https://hci.rwth-aachen.de/tiki-download_wiki_attachment.php?attId=2292 http://arduino.cc/en/Main/Products; Retrieved September 2014 http://www.freetronics.com/pages/stacking-arduino-shields http://playground.arduino.cc/ http://arstechnica.com/information-technology/2013/10/arduino-creator-explains-why-open-source-matters-in-hardware-too http://www.heise.de/newsticker/meldung/Arduino-gegen-Arduino-Gruender-streiten-um-die-Firma-2549653.html
Google Glass	https://support.google.com/glass/answer/3064131?hl=en http://www.pcmag.com/article2/0,2817,2416488,00.asp http://www.techinsights.com/teardown.com/google-glass/ http://www.forbes.com/sites/quora/2012/07/06/what-could-be-interesting-use-cases-for-google-glass/3/ https://developers.google.com/glass/ https://developers.google.com/glass/develop/gdk/ https://developers.google.com/glass/design/patterns
Project Ara	http://www.projectara.com/faq/ http://time.com/10115/google-project-ara-modular-smartphone/ http://www.technologyreview.com/news/525386/why-googles-modular-smartphone-might-actually-succeed/ http://www.theverge.com/2014/4/15/5615880/building-blocks-how-project-ara-is-reinventing-the-smartphone http://www.wired.com/2014/10/day-with-project-ara/
SmartThings	http://time.com/3117493/samsung-home-automation-smartthings/ http://thenextweb.com/insider/2014/05/21/smartthings-officially-launches-connected-home-platform-new-certification-program/ http://www.slashgear.com/smartthings-review-living-in-the-smart-home-17341453/ http://www.cnet.com/news/smart-home-showdown-wink-vs-smartthings/ https://ifttt.com/smartthings http://docs.smartthings.com/en/latest/device-type-developers-guide/ http://docs.smartthings.com/en/latest/introduction/
LEGO Mind-storms	http://www.lego.com/de-de/mindstorms/support/faq/ http://makezine.com/2013/08/02/lego-mindstorms-ev3-source-code-available/

	https://github.com/mindboards/ev3sources http://brickinthecloud.com/2013/11/14/programming-the-new-lego-mindstorms-ev3/
Prosyst	http://www.continuaalliance.org/about-the-alliance https://standards.ieee.org/findstds/standard/healthcare_it.html
John Deere	http://www.iso.org/iso/iso_catalogue/catalogue_tc/catalogue_detail.htm?csnumber=54390
RACE	http://www.projekt-race.de/upload/downloads/PI_Race_2013-02-20.pdf
OpenXC	http://openxcplatform.com/host-devices/hardware.html http://openxcplatform.com/overview/index.html http://openxcplatform.com/overview/faq.html http://techcrunch.com/2013/01/08/ford-launches-its-openxc-sdk-and-hardware-specs-to-let-developers-access-its-cars-sensors-and-metrics/
AutoPNP	http://www.autopnp.com/

Annex B   Communication of the research

The publications listed below are the work of the author of this dissertation in collaboration with doctoral research fellows and supervisors. Table 22 contains all the previous publications of the author that revealed parts of this thesis and the major overlaps with it as well as the author's main contributions to the paper

Table 23   Overview of the author's contribution in each publication

Publication	Relevant Content
(Soeldner et al. 2012)	An earlier version of part III, 2 (first study) was published as a paper and presented at the conference "Gemeinschaften in Neuen Medien" (GeNeMe) 2012. The publication can be found in the conference's proceedings. It was developed further using comments made by editors and reviewers of the conference. I substantially contributed to all the aspects of both the initial and the current version of the paper, including the theory review, literature selection, conceptual elaboration and the results gained
(Soeldner et al. 2013)	An earlier version of part III, 3 (second study) was published as a paper and presented at the "Americas Conference on Information Systems (AMCIS) 2013". The publication can be found in the conference's proceedings. It was developed further using comments made by editors and reviewers of the conference. I substantially contributed to all the aspects of both the initial and the current version of the paper, including the theory review, literature selection, data collection and analysis and interpretation of the results gained
(Soeldner, Roth, and Moeslein 2015)	An earlier version of part III, 4 (third study) was published as a paper and presented at the "Pacific Asia Conference on Information Systems (PACIS) 2015". The publication can be found in the conference's proceedings. It was developed further using comments made by editors and reviewers of the conference. I substantially contributed to all the

aspects of both the initial and the current version of the paper, including the theory review, literature selection, data collection and analysis and interpretation of the results gained